THE LOVE OF

Brian Walker

This book is dedicated to Pamela Rita Walker, my wife and lover, the mother and grandmother of our family. A woman who could spread happiness to many people, who could make people take her to their hearts and who could comfort people when they were down. I was an extremely fortunate man.

She is my inspiration, my desire, my eternal sweetheart! I will never stop loving her!

A special Thank You to my good mate Laurence Payne for his technical skills. His unlimited knowledge of publishing, of computer skills, and especially for his friendship when I needed it.

ThankYou to Travis Crowther for designing the cover and for his help and comfort.

Lastly, Thank You to Tony Locantro. He has not been involved in the production of this book, but he is always at hand when needed.

The majority of the photos in this story were taken by me, taken for no other reason than my belief that the subject of the pictures, my wife, Pam, was beautiful.

I thought, and still think that she had a rare kind of beauty. She had a natural elegance and poise. Her smile could light up a dark room and create a feeling of joy. It was never difficult to photograph her, perhaps because I was in awe of her beauty.

Also by Brian Walker:
Tales of the Old Iron Pot: Memoirs of an East End guttersnipe
Available on Amazon

Contents

Foreword

Make no mistake about it this is a Love Story. Perhaps this kind of story is out of date nowadays, but I have no doubt that love and romance will never die. This is about two very young kids from Hackney who fell in love at the tender age of Twelve, and in spite of shyness, eventually stayed in love until they were Eighty-Two. The main Character in this tale is my wife and mother of our children. She had a magical charm about her, elegance and beauty, kindness, understanding and a unique style of dressing. As she often quoted 'I am not interested in fashion, Just 'Style'. Just as well because she had it in large amounts.

When I decided to write about my love and infatuation for my wife Pam, I could not decide what this book should be called. I thought that the title should show my love for her and her dignity. Modern words are fine, but they do not express exactly what I feel. Some people suggested that I call it *'My Rock'* but there was nothing hard and cold about her. I had it suggested that the name should be *'My Best Friend'*, but that sounds like a title you should apply to a dog. Then I cast my mind back to the days when people said what they really meant, I chose a phrase that is not trendy, but is to the point. It is also satisfying, so I am calling it *'THE LOVE OF MY LIFE'*.

THE LOVE OF MY LIFE

Chapter 1. Granny Knots and Woggles

When I reached the age of twelve, I was pretty pleased with myself. I was enjoying school and getting a thrill out of learning. Only a year before I became top of my class in my primary school and as a result, I passed my matriculation and I found myself in one of East London's best schools. What's more I could not get enough of the new knowledge that was being taught so when the results of our year's work and of the first year's exams were announced, I was once again top of the class in this prestigious, historic school making my Mum and Dad so proud of me and telling me and everyone else that one day I would be 'The Prime Minister', I was now so full of myself.

I had already joined the Boy Scouts and became just as eager to learn about scouting. I learnt how to tie very complicated knots, to identify all sorts of trees, to track wildlife and to identify animals by looking at the footprints left in the mud by horses, deer, foxes, wolves, badgers and birds. We even learnt how to identify some species by their droppings. Of course, we learnt how to make shelters from half a dozen branches of a tree, to start a fire and cook over a campfire and very importantly to dig a latrine pit. All this knowledge seemed irrelevant because we never saw many trees, not many birds and no such thing as a deer and, definitely not even a whiff of these exotic droppings.

You see, this was just after the war that had raged for six years and had flattened large tracts of East London and frightened away most of the wildlife. Our wide-open spaces were made up of bomb craters and demolished buildings. It was about then that I became disenchanted with tying knots that I had no use for and polishing my woggle every night - it had become a disappointing chore.

Believe it or not, I was just a bit shy of the opposite sex and I had a dislike of girls, or perhaps it was an excuse for my shyness. At our primary school we had a music master who insisted that we should all learn to dance so he played waltzes, foxtrots and other close quarter dances, he would tell us all to pick someone of the opposite sex to dance with, this order made a chill run down my spine, and there would be a dithering group of pupils who were reluctant to even think of such an intimate encounter with a female. I had the advantage of having my cousin Audrey in the same class as me and dear little Audrey was destined to save my embarrassment week after week, but my dislike of girls still remained.

Well, let's face it, they were soppy, snivelly and giggly, especially when a boy passed by and they gathered in a tight bunch putting their heads together and mumbled, it was then that the mumble became a loud shrieking scream leaving us baffled boys wondering just what exactly was going on. And another thing, they had a strange smell about them, and they went on and on about such strange potions as *California Poppy* and *Phul-Nana* and were forever sniffing at each other's necks and smiling like satisfied cats.

At that time we lived in a flat with a back yard that was sunk below the level of a block of maisonettes and gave the occupants a clear view of me and my family and what's more gave us a front row view of the goings on in the area of the entrance to the maisonettes. In this entrance there was frequently a group of these strange creatures who looked at me in a detailed way making me cringe and hastily retreat into our little flat with a red face and an uneasy and defeated feeling about myself.

On one occasion there was about a dozen of these female nuisances sitting on the step of the entrance. They were squealing and chattering and huddled like a clutch of baby birds seeking warmth from each other. In contempt I turned my back on them but as I spun round, I spotted something that was to alter my life. Somewhere in the middle of these nestlings was a small, delicate and pretty little face that I had never seen before. Immediately my heart started thumping and I found it hard to breathe, my head spun, and I became dizzy. It felt like I had been hit over the head. I hadn't realised at that moment, but I was suffering from a bad case of 'LOVE at first sight'. It seems that Cupid had shot me, not with his arrow but with double-barrelled shotgun. But I was only twelve and I didn't even know who this lovely creature was, and what's more, what did I know of matters of the heart? So, I did the only thing that I could think of, I went indoors and flopped into an armchair and shut my eyes and tried to work out just what had happened to me.

Just then in came my mum and took one look at me and said "What's the matter with you? Are you alright?" She then put her hand on my forehead and said "You feel very hot! I had better give you a powder." That was her answer to every little ailment, but although I never agreed she unwrapped the flimsy bit of paper that held the universal answer to all ailments, Beecham's Powder, and shook it into a glass of water. I, then lying through my teeth, agreed that it was miraculous and swallowed the strange tasting concoction in one gulp. "There you are" said Mum looking pleased with herself "You feel better already, don't you?" I never dared to say no or to tell her that I was infatuated with a girl that I never knew. But I just couldn't get this dainty girl from my mind!

So there was nothing else to do but to summon up all my courage and talk to this delicate person who had captivated me, so the next time these chattering nest mates settled down on the step I casually stopped by and attempted to say hello but nothing came out of my mouth so I simply stood there looking uneasy. In those days it was the custom for young boys to wear short trousers until they were about 13 or 14 and I was no exception, I stood in front of this Jury of females completely unaware of my bare knees, that is until one of the mouthier girls looked me straight in the face and brazenly said "You want to get some proper trousers, mate. The snow will be on the ground soon."

I wanted to say that I wore shorts all the year round, but it occurred to me that my shaky reply would only make me look more of a fool. Just then the object of my desire passed by and said, "Don't tease him, you are embarrassing him." Now her sympathetic nature spurred me on to ask her what her name was. "It's Pam" was her gentle reply and my trembly answer was "My name is Brian."

This was the very moment that I decided that helping old ladies across the road, taking stones out of horses hooves, granny knots and woggles, and even old Baden-Powell himself should remain in my childhood, from now on I would be a young man!

Pam with my Mum

Chapter 2. Hold My Hand

Now that I had actually spoken to and introduced myself to this lovely slip of a girl I felt just a little bit more able to talk to her, providing, of course that she didn't look me straight in the eye (I really was very shy).

Every Tuesday night a Picture Show was held in a local Community Hall. Films were shown by a local enthusiast, he had a big, clumsy, projector which was carried in his large station wagon. It sounds very grand but the station wagon had to park outside and the poor old cinema fanatic would have to get the heavy, awkward equipment up two flights of stairs. This is where the 'fun' began. Our fun was certainly not fun for this local fan of Hollywood, he cursed and grunted and eventually shouted at the ignorant rabble who were getting great entertainment by mocking him before the show began. This was only the start of the mayhem.

Although this noisy, unruly behavior nearly drove this well-meaning Hollywood fan to an early grave, it was very convenient for us would-be sweethearts. Because as soon as the projector started and flickered its light around the hall the baying mob would express their feelings about the ancient offerings that were laid before us. Of course, they must have been dragged from the depths of the 'not wanted' cupboard of the Film Museum. Sometimes we were lucky enough to get some creaky, flickering Western - like the very popular 'Hopalong Cassidy'. Although this yobbery nearly drove the Hollywood fan to an early grave, it was very convenient for would be sweethearts.

Whilst all the audience who were not at all interested in the films, were having fun shouting, swearing, fighting and rearranging the furniture, us of a more romantic nature somehow squeezed into the corner of the back row and became oblivious of the bad behaviour and concentrated on, "going-out" with each other. With all the riotous, noisy ruckus going on hiding my youthful shyness I took a deep nervous breath and blurted out to the object of my desire "Can I sit with you?" She never said a word in answer to my shaky question but simply squeezed up to leave a space for me to sit with her.

My knees trembled as we got over our nerves and concentrated on 'going-out' with each other, which in our case it was nervously holding hands and saying nothing! The only excitement was when "Old Hoppy" would leap from his horse and put the 'Baddies' in jail. Then an even noisier and longer cheer would go up causing us to

squeeze hands even harder and at last look into each other's eyes. - Ah, Bliss!

Both me and the lovely Pam lived in the same street, but it never occurred to me to walk her home. She joined her nest mates and I united with my mates who were now laughing at the projectionist dangerously descending the suicidal staircase. Just a lingering look at each other, then off to our homes.

By now I was deeply 'in love' with her, but never had the nerve to say anything about it. I had a slight feeling that she was looking for something more committal from me but I didn't know what to do, there was no-one that I could ask, but looking back through more experience eyes, I can see that she wanted me to kiss her.

Three-or-four times a year a big fair visited the river bank near where we lived, as well as all the thrilling rides and freak shows, unlicensed traders would sell small objects and gifts from their suit-cases and I decided that a beautiful gift would please her and would give her a hint about how I thought of her. One of the fly-by-night merchants made and sold name brooches. By twisting shiny copper wire into names and fixing a pin on the back he produced nice little gifts fit for anyone's favourite loved one. I ran my eyes along the row of names and there twinkling at me was the very name 'Pamela' I thought that I would buy her this precious memento of our love, but then thought that she may laugh at such a gift so I went home. After a night of indecision, the next day I ran to the fair to buy this token of love for the girl who was occupying my thoughts every hour of the day.

I put it safely into my pocket and held it tight feeling very pleased with myself, but when I got it home and looked at it I felt that it was not suitable for someone as special as Pam or that the twittering nest mates would laugh at this tasteless, stupid gift, so I decided that I wouldn't show it to her. I had a feeling of regret and a hope that we might finish up together.

I realised that we were just a couple of love-sick kids.

I went home and took the copper brooch from my pocket went to the river bank and after a few minutes of thought dropped it into the murky water, as it slowly went to the bottom, the shiny copper twinkled less and less and

the precious brooch reached and finally sank into the mud. I never ever mentioned this childish but sincere action to Pam. We now saw less and less of each other and I realised that the flame of love was flickering out. But it never died in my heart, I still had yearnings and dreams that we would grow old together.

Chapter 3. The parting of the ways

There was never a vibrant or even an argumentative finish to the love affair, we simply stopped going out together. Of course, I was not pleased. Just how Pam felt I never knew. I felt a bit sad for a short time and soon the matter was forgotten. Or was it? I still had dreams and feelings for her.

The world was changing and the Teddy Boy fashion took over. As well as the clothing the attitude of being good boys dwindled and a spirit of Rebellion replaced it. I, like everyone else, became part of the local gang. I met a few girls and suddenly my shyness gradually disappeared as I became more mature. I had two regular girlfriends, when I say regular I mean that I saw them regularly once a week on Sunday evening to go to the local Picture Palace. Both were nice girls but nothing special, I soon got bored with them and the visits to cinema simply got lost and disappeared without a trace.

Then at the age of seventeen fate took a hand, helped enormously by my mum. One night I arrived home early from Gang duty and as I put my key in the lock there was a fumbling and suddenly the door was dragged open. There stood my Mum grinning from ear to ear and splurting out "Brian, there's someone to see you" and grabbing me and pulling me in said "I mean that Pammy's come to see me" Then added to give her statement a bit more truthfulness "Well she came to see Eira" - my younger sister. I didn't believe a word of it, because I was staring at this vision of beauty that stood before me.

The pretty little nest mate was now a full-grown woman and her youthful prettiness was taken over by a goddess of beauty and elegance. She was using her trade-mark captivating smile and it certainly captivated me. I was again lost-for-words, but my old mum chatted on and asked me at least three times "Are you pleased to see her?" The answer was apparent as I stood there with a big soppy grin on my face and my eyes scrutinising this beautiful and appealing woman who stood oozing charm, style and class.

Mum offered her yet another cup of tea and my little sister buzzed around her in admiration watching every move that Pam made.

After they drank the tea my conniving mother said in a very obvious way "Come on Brian, it's getting late, you had better take Pammy home", although she only lived across the road Mum made it sound as if it was a dangerous and perilous journey into the unknown.

Pam lived on the top floor of dark and scary block that had a gloomy and dark granite stairway. This made mum say, "Take her right to the top, don't let her walk up those awful stairs on her own" As if I would!

We slowly trudged up that gloomy stairway, taking our time simply to spend a little more time together. At the top of the stairs we talked together and it was so plain that we both wanted to be just a bit more than friends but again I was a bit too shy to make a move, that is until I had a talk with myself and said goodnight to her.

We both leaned together to have a peck on the cheek but changed our minds as we got close, we clutched each other and went into a full passionate embrace. At last our lips touched. It was glorious, we never rushed it, after all it had been a long time coming. Oh, heavenly feelings, our first grown up kiss and the start of a lifetime together, my heart beat like it had never done before. I had a feeling that Pam felt the same way too.

As I descended those awful stairs I turned back and boldly said "What are you doing tomorrow night?" There was a silent moment as she considered the loaded question and simply replied "Nothing much." Now full of confidence I boldly said "Right, I'll see you then". I floated down those dreaded stairs as if I was Fred Astaire. When I reached the ground floor I looked up and of course she was looking down at me with her wonderful smile making my head spin and my heart to miss a beat.

That was the end of the Teddy Boys, they were dumped in the same place as the scouts.

At this time, I realised that I had in fact, been in love with her from the very beginning, even when I was just 12 years old but I wasn't old enough to know it. Now I was sure! I swore to myself to protect her, to adore her. I placed her on a pedestal and worshipped her. When we went out together I made sure that I walked on the side of the pavement near the road and when we got on or off of a bus I very gentlemanly helped her on and off of the platform. She never

said anything about this somewhat old-fashioned behaviour, but I could see that she loved all the special attention that I gave her. I never stopped treating her like this.

Chapter 4. Making up for lost time

The following evening there was a delicate knock on our door, I knew exactly who it was and I couldn't get to the door quickly enough. I was not disappointed because standing on the doorstep, oozing beauty and sweetness was Pam, smiling as usual and having all the right effects on me.

"Do you fancy a walk?" I asked. The answer was obvious, so off we went strolling along the towpath of the River Lea, through the wood yards, pubs, and rickety buildings completely ignoring the many smells and scraps of timber that were strewn about. None of this mattered because we were in a world of romance, love and hope for the future. Those dreadful, gloomy granite stairs took even longer to climb and it took even longer to say goodnight.

We had many more of these magical moments over the next few weeks, each walk making me fall even deeper in love with my dream of delight.

She was genuinely captivating and kind, as I was soon to find out. As we walked one sunny evening we stopped to see an old man pruning the beautiful roses that grew on a tiny strip of land that he had made into an allotment. Pam could not help but say "those roses are so beautiful." The old chap stood up rather stiffly and asked her in a charming way "Would you like one young lady?" He was obviously under the spell of her youthful beauty as his gnarled hands reached into the pocket of his rather worn dungarees and produced an ancient pair of secateurs and carefully selected the best bloom and gently snipped it off.

He then gently handed the precious rose to Pam looking so pleased with himself, Pam was very pleased too. She thanked him profusely, the pair of them were so contented and full of mutual kindness. As we walked away, he stayed looking at us just to make the most of this pleasant moment.

Incidents such as this happened frequently confirming to me just what a special person she was, I was hooked!

We spent all our spare time together falling deeper and deeper in love. At that time, we both worked in Dalston just around the corner from one another, we spent our lunchtimes together and of course took the bus ride to work together. She always wore very stylish clothes, even lace gloves fixed at the wrist by a pearl button, people would ask me if she was a model. We sat together on the bus and I liked to hold her hand, but the lace felt like it was keeping us apart. On the very first day I simply slipped the pearl button through the buttonhole and held her delicate, smooth, warm hand. I held my breath as it reminded me of us holding hands in the riotous picture club in the Community Hall. Holding hands then became our way of showing how much we loved each other. A practice that would last for ever.

I took her to places that she had never been before. In Wood Green there was a pub called 'The Fishmonger's Arms'. At the back of the pub was a hall where Jazz nights were staged, the performers were at that time unknown but went on to be legends. I asked Pam if she would like to go there and she couldn't wait for Sunday night and showed a lot of enthusiasm for this minority style of entertainment. The venue attracted all kinds of people, Teddy Boys, college students, young music fans and one or two older fans who had admired this style of music from their youth.

Pam absolutely loved the somewhat mixed audience and so started a lifelong interest, no, not Jazz- but People Watching! To be fair, there were some sights to behold and we did have some fun guessing what kind of partners they had, what they worked as and most importantly - where did they get those bizarre but stylish clothes. With the bar selling scrumpy cider at sixpence-a-pint the guesses got wilder and more ridiculous and our laughter got louder. To be fair to Pam she never was rude about anyone, she simply made allowances for their odd behaviour and dress.

On the way home we took the underground, it was so packed that Pam had to sit at one end of the long coach, and I sat at the other end. I remember so clearly that she wore a very becoming bright red Beret that she pulled down to one side at the most attractive angle, she always had impeccable style so I couldn't stop looking at her.

As I stretched my neck to admire her a bit more, she gave me one of her smiles that could melt the hardest of hearts. I could see that most of the passengers were staring at her too, who could blame them! Her glamour and loveliness filled that long carriage and certainly reached me.

Chapter 5. Afloat in a boat

We were both lucky to live within feet of Middlesex Wharf, a delightful place despite the industry that settled around it. First of all, dominating the area, was the mighty James Latham's Timber Yard, with its loading sheds where all the finished timber was loaded onto the barges and shipped off to who knows where. The wharf, or what was left of it after the air raids, comprised of a row of cottages that were long abandoned and fly squatted. One enterprising businessman had moved into one old house and yard, and used them to cut up the wood from the many bomb damaged houses, then chop them up into kindling sticks and sell them to many shops in East London. Then there was one derelict house that pigs were kept in and in return for a few buckets of swill and a warm space, they filled the area with their unique smell.

The river was also smelly and full of rubbish that would turn you off of your dinner. Not the best setting for a love story, but love is blind they say and probably has no sense of smell either. Despite the disadvantages the area had many attractive advantages too. Just step over the footbridge and you were on the green and lush Marshes, Millfields lay on our side of the river and the lovely Springfield Park was a ten-minute walk away. But the best attraction were the numerous boat yards that were situated just feet from our doors. You just had to call in and ask for a boat and it was there for you.

Many sunny afternoons Pam and me would step into a rowing boat and lose ourselves in a romantic moment, ignoring many smells and floating rubbish. At one spot a little further up the river was a quiet spot where a large tree had spread out and conveniently provided a shaded area that no-one on the other bank could see. I always felt tired when we approached it, I just had to take a rest at this destination and would join Pam in the large rear seat and whisper sweet nothings and share a kiss or two, or three, whose counting? Pam's fragrance and beauty overcame all the disadvantages.

There were many examples of admiration from strangers and a lot more from me, I would sit and stare at Pam in disbelief of her angelic looks and poise, then I would look into the mirror and wonder what she saw in me.

Chapter 6. Off to do my duty!

Over the next year we fell even deeper in love, I was by now infatu-ated with her, my family and friends shared my admiration for her, everything was going swimmingly when suddenly along came some-thing to spoil our blissful happiness, through my letter box came a brown envelope, I knew exactly what it was.... It was my call up papers summoning me to join in all the fun and to become a soldier!

We carried on with our passionate love enjoying every moment but one day the inevitable order came through the post. I was to report to Oswestry in Shropshire on December the Sixth. Pam was upset, I was excited, but my old Dad was fuming. "Why do they want you to go in before Christmas? They might as well have called you up after the holiday" Then in an unprecedented angry way, "I will write to them and offer to take your place" Of course I told him not to be silly. He just mumbled to himself.

The dreaded day arrived, Pam was sad, my Dad was still complain-ing, my Mum was dabbing her eyes with her hanky and I was look-ing forward to unknown adventures, but course I couldn't admit it. Pam accompanied me to Paddington Station to say goodbye in her special way, she had already bought me the ultimate in travel gear, the latest fashion, that I had never seen before, a hold-all! In the hold-all she had packed sandwiches, chocolate and again the latest thing in catering, a can of beer! It was the first one that I ever seen, somehow in some strange way it made me realise just how much she cared for me.

On the platform at Paddington Station, standing by with their nearest and dearest, was a large cluster of young men. There were posh fellows, rough fellows, noisy men, quiet men and a large contingent of Teddy Boys, all waiting to tell the British Army that they were not going to be bossed about by anyone. Then an army truck arrived and parked on the platform, out stepped four big Military Policemen with the peaks of their caps pulled down onto their busted noses, they gave one shout and all the rebelliousness melted away as we all scuffled to get on the train without saying a word. The engine's whistle blew as it pulled away. I looked out of the window, through the steam, to see Pam with her hanky to her gorgeous face.

She was so sad because we wouldn't see each other for a long time and Xmas would be lonely this year. But fate took a hand and things turned out to be more favourable.

We stayed at Oswestry for just two weeks in order to get kitted out and then transferred to a proper training camp in order to be trained as real fighting men.

We arrived at Tonfanau, a large camp in a small place on the remote West Coast of Wales, as we stepped down from the train we looked at the bleak mountains and crossed our fingers. The dark clouds released their cargo of snow, it was bloody freezing. Now we would never see Christmas at home, but the Welsh weather, a cranky old engine and a kind-hearted old Jewish cab driver were to be our good fairies this year.

It was announced that the temperature had dropped so much that the plumbing had frozen and that we would all be sent home for Christmas.

After a quick cuppa and a few soggy sandwiches, we were on our way back to Paddington. The army camp had its own station and in a short time most of the personnel were crammed into the overloaded train and our perilous and uncomfortable journey began when the crowed train chuffed on its way yet again. We were headed for dear old Paddington again dropping off soldiers on the way. Thirteen hours later we almost chugged into our destination. After all that time without a toilet, we were desperate. I will let you use your imagination about how we managed. I say almost because the train, for some reason, stopped about a few hundred yards from the platform and stood still for another half an hour. The impatient squaddies rebelled, they jumped from the carriages and walked along the

15

railway lines. Of course the Military police stood in our way, but the now exasperated would-be soldiers just ignored them. The air was now blue with good old British Army language.

I gave a sigh of relief because my uncomfortable journey was almost over, I couldn't wait to see and hold my loved one, but all problems were not yet resolved. It was now 2 o'clock in the morning and we had to get across London, I went to the cab rank, but the cabbies didn't want to go so far or wanted a fortune to get us home.

Just then a cab pulled to the front of the pick-up point and an old, very Jewish driver stuck his head out of the window and said "Where are you going, lads?" I said tentatively "East London?", our 'Knight without shining armour' simply said "Jump in". He then headed our way dropping my companions off at various points chatting as he went. I was the last one to be left in the cab and said that I wanted to go to Lea Bridge. He said "OK. I'm going home now, so I'm going your way."

When we arrived at Lea Bridge I asked our hero how much did he want, I had called the cab so was prepared to pay for all my newly found mates, but this unexcitable, genial old Eastender simply said "I wouldn't take anything from you, I was a soldier myself once". I thanked him and wished him a Merry Christmas and he replied "Mazel Tov". I have never forgotten this kind-hearted old soldier.

Early that morning I called on Pam, she was still in bed and was surprised and extremely glad to see me. Aware that she wasn't as immaculately dressed as she normally would be, she said "I must look awful". Not a bit, it was the best Christmas that we ever had.

Within a few days, the plumbing problems at Tonfanau were resolved. We reluctantly dragged our heels back to the Valley of Wind and Rain and to the shouting and humiliating behaviour of the training instructors. Now it was apparent that the festive season, the frozen pipes and all were over, it was now soldiering at its worst. I could take the marching, rifle drill, and standing in the bitter Welsh weather. What I didn't like was the absence of Pam, her beauty and her warm and loving goodnights. We had no choice but to soldier on and after another six weeks we were pronounced proper fighting men, but I never wanted to fight anyone, I just wanted to be back in the arms of my love.

Now came the uncertainty of the postings. Most of my fellow trainees were from London and wanted a posting within reach of their loving homes, a lot of the South Londoners preferred places like Woolwich, Kent or the South Coast. The postings were announced to the incredibly nervous men and my name, that of course started with W, was the last to be announced. Most of the men were happy with their postings and when my posting was called out, they were gasps from the home loving squaddies, I was off to... Hong Kong!

I was Happy to be having some Far Eastern adventures but heart-broken to not being able to see my delicious Pam for nearly two years. But first a bit of Home Leave. After two weeks of passion, tears and vows to be faithful, I set sail for the mysterious East.

Of course, there were no 'phones, Wi-Fi or even carrier pigeons, just a fortnightly letter and pen-written love vows, but our love for each other kept well and truly alive. There were certainly no luxury liners to transport us to our land of dreams, Hong Kong. Just a large old ex-German Troop ship with small bunks stacked up to the ceiling, the descent from which threatened to break your leg every time we got out of bed half asleep. When our ship eventually entered Hong Kong harbour most of the servicemen were silent, they were too busy taking in the Oriental beauty of the colony.

After a very eventful year in the Colony, the War Office decided that a cut in the number of servicemen was necessary and that we would all be returning to the UK. There were mixed feelings amongst the men including me but after a short month we sailed from Kowloon set for Southampton, this time by way of a different route. We saw many sights, a very eventful journey! (I won't give details, there may be another book here.)

Chapter 7. Back where I belong!

After a long and laborious journey that had taken me around the world I finally arrived at Clapton Station, now I knew that I was in reach of just what I had yearned for from the other side of the world.

I was overloaded with Army Equipment, presents and civilian clothes that bought in that far off corner of the Empire, very nice, very exotic, but so bloody difficult to carry. Just then a railway porter arrived, he was bedecked with a chest-full of medals. I recognised him, only a year or two before he had threatened to knock my bloody head off and dared me to fight him, all because I was a Teddy Boy. Now he was so helpful and admiring of me. "Don't struggle with all that lot, take all your presents home then come back for the rest whenever you want to" I thanked him and my old adversary just said "Glad to see you back" and shook my hand! Then with the precious gifts on my shoulder I marched down the hill to be in the bosom of my family and into the arms of my special love.

When I reached the bottom of the hill and turned the corner into our little street of terraced houses, I looked about for the Brass Band to greet me. No such luck. It was as quiet as a grave, but as I neared our flat the door burst open revealing a small crowd of relatives, neighbours and a couple of gate crashers, but where was my precious Pam? I looked around the tightly packed crowd but no Pam, that is until I waded through the well-wishers, all keen to kiss me and hold me, and found her standing in the corner as quiet as a mouse and looking coy. I gave her a kiss and asked her "Why are you hiding away?" Her simple answer made me blush and realise just how I felt about her, "I'm shy, I haven't seen you for so long" I had a tear in my eye as I kissed and kissed her.

For the next three weeks I was on Embarkation Leave and lavished all my time on her and our strengthened love.

Far too quickly those three weeks passed by and I was off again, this time not quite so far away, I was sent to Pembrokeshire, West Wales.

I joined a new regiment in Pembroke Dock and now being a seasoned soldier, I soon settled in. This part of the British Isles is beautiful and charming and I wrote to Pam saying that when I could I would love to take her to the romantic and historic town of Tenby. She replied by saying that she would be thrilled to go as she had never been on holiday before. Now I was determined to fulfil the promise, you see I was aware of her lack of travel because her mother was an alcoholic and noted for her craving for beer so most of the housekeeping money rarely reached the household. Pam had four sisters, two of them just small kids and she made sure that babies of the family were looked after and clothed decently. This made me more obliged to give her the holidays that she had missed.

However there was the rest of my Army Service to complete. Because of the exciting scenery and the seaside atmosphere the time flew by helped of course by our weekly, passionate love letters. I did at one time, just once, get a long weekend Pass. A long weekend pass didn't seem enough, it was for four days and seeing that it included travelling time it meant that we only had two short days together. I jumped on the train at Pembroke Dock and settled down for the long tedious journey to Paddington and beyond. After what seemed an eternity I arrived at Clapton Station. All the long way from the western extremities of the British Isles I thought of nothing but the delicious Pam. I wondered if she would be waiting at the station for me or would our very shaky method of communication let us down? By the time I stepped down from the train I was so excited and longing to hold her, I climbed the stairs to street level, turned the corner and there she was, framed by the door to the station. My heart thumped and my knees knocked as she gave me one of her special smiles, I wanted to tell her that I had missed her so much and that she looked even more beautiful than the last time that I saw her, but she was dying to tell me all the local news, who was seeing who, about just who had fallen out with who and such trivialities. I just could not get a word in so this called for direct action, as we passed the first shop doorway I grabbed her arm, pulled her in to the privacy of the shopfront and kissed her passionately. She tried her best to continue her scandal report but because of my efforts she got the idea of what special moment was all about and gradually stopped talking and joined in with this stolen moment of passionate love. I can't remember how long we stayed in the doorway but I do recall that we stopped at least three times on the walk to my Mum's home. Of course when my Mum saw Pam she started telling her all the very same gossip that I had just heard, they spoke of Pam's clothes, who was getting married, who was pregnant and almost anything that kept us two lovebirds apart. After the third cup of tea my very understanding Mum went into the kitchen and as she closed the door lowered her voice and said "I'll leave you alone so that you can say Hello to each other properly". We didn't want to upset my Mum so we did as we were told. There was no need to upset her, was there?

Finally the December date for the resumption of my civilian life was upon me, it was a shock even though I had been waiting for it for the last two years.

I can honestly say that I did not regret one day of my Army service, I had adventures, travel and the security of my fellow soldiers. I had the time of my life, but I had to be careful about saying that to Pam because she suspiciously would say "Why what did you get up to?"

I arrived home to a less exciting welcome than last time, there were no hordes of friends and relations filling our little front room, just me and Pam and a longing to make up for my absence...

Chapter 8. Civvy Street

I had my first day as a civilian on Thursday, found myself a job on Friday and started my new job on Monday and soon pay day came around. It felt so good to hold an envelope with £10 in it, we only got about £1.50 from H.M. the Queen, so this vast amount of cash set my head thinking of my promise to take Pam on a holiday. So with the help of the Never-Never system and an imagination that had no limits, I set off to buy a vehicle that would waft us away into the Mysterious West- Wales!

I soon found a lovely little van that Pam described as "Ooh, cosy" So here we were, a bit of money, a nice van, and thoughts of exploring unheard of places. All was in place for romantic adventures, but one thing stood in our way... I couldn't drive!

A good mate came to our rescue, he offered to give me lessons after work and on weekends, but all this driving business was harder than it looked, so progress was slow, making me disappointed and frustrated and Pam asking "How are you getting on?" made me even grumpier than usual. Never daunted, I applied for a driving test and was promised a date in late August dashing our hopes for a holiday that year. However by about July we were longing for an adventure so I announced myself 'Ready to Drive', Pam was fearful, my mum could see nothing but a disaster befalling us and I, hiding my many doubts, was annoyingly full of myself again. My 'down to earth' dad for once was showing signs of being scared for our safety. And when my mum looked into the tiny interior of our "Ooh, cosy" van and asked in a very concerned way, "Where will you sleep?" I pointed to the back of the van, which now looked even tinier and said "There" This is when my mum's Welsh Chapel upbringing burst forth, "But you are not married" she said. We both laughed but mum stormed off to consult some Celtic God. But the situation was the same, no driving licence, no wedding certificate, no experience of distance driving, but lots of shaky confidence, a bit of East End Bravado and an aching desire to take my gorgeous Pam on her first ever holiday!

Pam was very excited and prepared all her stylish clothes and shoes and carefully packed them into a large case, but when I saw this huge case my heart dropped. Rather angrily, I said "Where do you think that 'Coffin' is going to be packed?" She gave me one of her 'little girl in trouble looks' as I noisily pushed the lump of unnecessary cargo into the small space in the van. I felt relieved to have loaded all our equipment when the 'little girl' asked "What about these?"

In her hand she held two bags full of 'bits and pieces'. My angry reply was "Stick them where you like" And she did! Socks, towels, pillows and all those annoying things that women like to take with them were stuffed down the backs of the seats, behind the spare wheel and other such places. I grumpily said "Come on now, it's bedtime".

Chapter 9. Into the unknown

Very early the next morning we set off on what turned out to be the first of many adventures that we would have in our long life together. As it was my first long distance trip I was feeling apprehensive and pretty daring at the same time, so there was no use in hanging about so I simply started the engine and set off on the road to who knows where. Pam looked just a bit nervous, but then she was always just a bit nervous!

Way back in those far off days there were no such thing as motorways or service stations, but not to worry I had my faithful, well-thumbed *AA Members Handbook* that I had bought on a second hand stall in the market, so I followed the road that lead to North Wales, it was the A5, a long and tedious route.

Within a short time, we crossed the North Circular road and I felt so good, my Boy Scout days had given me the gift of map reading and we felt relaxed at last. What I never knew was that the A5 went right through the centre of Birmingham, passing places that we had never heard of, scaring the life out of me and wanting me to throw that bloody AA book out of the window.

Eventually we left the northern boundary of Brum and we spotted a real good old fashioned lorry drivers Caff! Inside it was smoky and noisy but what did we care? They served the thickest, tastiest Bacon Rolls and hot tea. Pam was delighted and got stuck into the succulent breakfast surrounded by the admiring lorry drivers.

As we left the *'Oasis of Greasy Nosh'* Pam fluttered her eyes and said that she felt a bit tired, so I told her to have a five-minute snooze while I drove on. She immediately closed her eyes and never opened them until we reached North Wales asking "Have I been to sleep?" This was to be her usual routine for all the many journeys that we made in the British Isles and Europe for years to come. She must have slept through some of the most beautiful scenery in Europe!

We finally arrived at Bettws-Y-Coed and pitched our van next to a rippling river. A little-known acquaintance had generously lent us a 'nice tent'. "It is an ex-army tent" he assured me, I could see that he wasn't lying because the so called solid tent was full of large bullet holes, and it had enough mud on it to repair a duck pond and it stank like a rotten cabbage. Pam took one look at this tent that looked like it was last used by The Eighth Army, and staring in disgust said " I'm not sleeping in that filthy thing, Didn't you look at it before you accepted it?" So I reluctantly took the massive case out of the van and placed it in drivers cab, we took a lot of the bits and pieces and 'lost' them, then squeezed into the back of the tiny van. It was very tight, but... we managed!

Next day we had an eye-opening tour of Snowdonia, she squealed with delight at the towering mountains and the thrilling waterfalls, but she was clearly not used to being out of London. When I remarked that she should hold tight because we were about to go up a steep mountain she said, sitting back at a 45-degree angle, "Are we going up yet?" Later we were driving along a road that overlooked a field full of bulrushes she was amazed to see 'wild elephants' pushing through the tall plants. Of course there were no elephants, just rain-soaked cows!

Perhaps the funniest mistake that became a joke in the family for years was when we were trying to pronounce the puzzling welsh town names. She said "That's a funny name, '*Goslow*' doesn't sound very Welsh". It was a roughly painted sign near a roadworks telling the traffic to GO SLOW. We both laughed at these silly gaffes, especially Pam. She was always able to laugh at herself, no false pride about her, she was so special. She openly admitted to being 'scatty' and found it hilarious.

I took her to the tops of the highest mountains, down to the sandiest beaches and rode on the small steam railways, she said that it was the best holiday that she had ever had. I had to remind her that it was the only one.

Later that year I passed my driving test and we had a lot of trips to the coast taking Pam's two younger sisters, Patti and Janice with us, the weather that year was very hot and sunny so our cosy little van had its work cut out, taking us all to the seaside and doubling up as bedroom for Patti and Janice on the way home. On one journey home Pam slipped into the back and cuddled up with her two little sisters, waking up only when we arrived back in Hackney.

Early in the next year we eventually finished up in in the much-desired Tenby. She was delighted and managed to 'Ooh and aah' her way around the little lanes and alleyways. We dined in most of the restaurants, and of course she looked like a film star in her expensive clothes. Actually, she bought most of them in Roman Road Market. Looking at her at her in all her finery, one thought came to my head "So that's why she wanted that bloody great case."

After that wonderful week of adventures we got home and out of the blue... she proposed to me!

That took the wind right out of my sails, I hadn't expected it, but I just took one look at her and my mind was made up, what else could I say but 'Yes!'

But this made a hole in our plans for more adventures, I had to sell the van and concentrate on saving for the wedding.

Pam decided to save money by making the dresses for all four bridesmaids and to make the bouquets. She had previously made dresses for herself and for her two younger sisters, very successfully, sewing them all by hand because she never had a sewing machine and was about to make the wedding outfits for our wedding when my mum said "I've got a machine, it's in our bedroom covered in our spare blankets" Into the bedroom went the two hopeful women and off came the blankets revealing an ancient treadle machine that would not have looked out of place in a museum. "You see, it's lovely!" said Mum brushing away the dust from it, "Just what we want!"

It was summertime and Pam set up her workshop in our tiny back yard and off she went creating an East End's version of haute-couture surrounded by the iron balconies, the tin baths hanging from nails in the wall, dad's pigeons fluttering about, and the neighbours hanging over the balconies shooing the pigeons away from the yards of immaculate white dress material. The event took a life of its own with neighbours making tea and cakes and offering advice while Dad struggled to keep his perfect little garden in order. I loved all the fuss and to-do! Of course, the central figure of this outdoor workshop was my lovely, talented and stylish Pam. I was so proud of her!

Chapter 10. Wedding

The months flew by and soon we were getting excited by the imminent wedding. We had booked the local church (just to please my Mum and her Welsh ancestors) and on the day the four bridesmaids looked adorable but of course the star of the event was the new Mrs. Walker. She was stunning and all friends, neighbours and family queued up to have their photos taken with her. If I remember rightly one particular couple wanted a photo with me, of course I obliged as they ran back to have another photo with the bride.

The wedding night was none of your business, but we both woke up very happy.

That week we had our Honeymoon in... Hackney. Well, we did have a day in Kew Gardens and a coach trip to the Wye Valley and of course we fitted in a day out to our favourite place, the lovely Epping Forest. It was April and the trees were turning green and the ferns were becoming lush and dense, so why waste the privacy that the undergrowth provided. We crept into the very natural boudoir and cuddled up to each other and were soon lost in the ecstasy of the love that we felt for each other. Suddenly I felt a hot breath upon my back and heard a loud snort, when I turned around I saw the strange sight of the inside of a horse's nostril and a long neck stretching out. My eyes followed the long neck until I could see that the horse had a rider on it's back, looking down his nose at us in a superior way was a forest Ranger, smartly dressed in a brown tweed jacket, highly polished leather gaiters and with a brown hat perched on his head. "Can I remind you that this is a public place and that there are other people about?" he said in a sarcastic, seen it all before kind of way. "But we are doing nothing wrong" I replied "Any way we are married!" I said in an innocent, butter wouldn't melt way. "Well why don't you go home to the privacy and comfort of your own home" he replied, we never wanted an argument, so that was just what we did!

We settled down to wedded bliss and our love for each other and our healthy desires kept us content. All this was in 1960 and by 1967 our healthy desires had produced three bouncing boys who were to be the best thing that had ever happened to us.

Of course Pam did what all good mothers did, she worried about them all the time and blamed me whenever they were poorly. One idle day I took our eldest boy, Glenn, then about four years old into the toilet and me still being a kid at heart taught him how to play 'sword fencing', you know, weeing together and trying to cross each other's flow. We were both laughing because we were being just a bit rude, when I noticed that Glenn's sword was rusty, his wee was very dark, almost like Cola. I called Pam who immediately became very concerned and without any hesitation took Glenn to the Doctor's Surgery that was conveniently situated just at the other end of our street. When she returned she wasn't very satisfied because the Doctor told her that it was nothing to be concerned about because there was not a normal colour for kid's urine. Then he added that "all you mums are the same. You worry about everything, so go home and see how he is tomorrow. "This was about half past five so we had dinner and settled down comfortably in front of the Telly when there was a knock on our door and there stood the Doctor looking very sheepish and with a letter in his hand. This was a report on the tests that were carried out on Glenn's wee, it appeared that he had a problem with his kidneys and that we should take him right away to the Children's Hospital in Hackney Road. Pam was by now absolutely a bundle of nerves and boldly told the Doctor that a mother's intuition was better than any medical learning, the poor old doctor was embarrassed and apologised again, before leaving.

Our second son, Billy was just a baby so Pam walked across the road to her sister Olive's house and left little Billy in Olive's care while we both took the very puzzled Glenn to the hospital where he was admitted. It was a very heart-breaking feeling seeing our little boy being admitted to this large ward. Pam held on to me with a very concerned look on her face, Glenn just took it all in his stride like it was some kind of adventure. Glenn was kept in the ward for nine weeks, a long time to be parted from our little boy. Pam visited Glenn every day with the daily help of her sister Olive, never once complaining about her extra burden, she was a perfect mother. When Glenn was eventually released from the hospital there were some advantages, Pam had always fussed over her kids, washing them, dressing them and generally waiting on them hand and foot, but now our little man could wash and dress himself and scrub his teeth relentlessly. The hospital routine had instilled these habits in him, we were so proud of him.

When our second son Bill was still very young, Pam was feeling just a bit under the weather. We had been sun worshiping as usual, she looked so tanned and healthy as normal but decided that she would visit the doctor. The doctor took one look at her and his diagnosis was that she had had too much of the sun and that everything would soon settle down and would be regular soon. But it turned out to be that she was pregnant with our third baby, Pam told us all that the doctor had decided that she had partaken of too much sun, my old dad remarked "Yes, too much of my son." In a short time we had three bonny boys and a lifetime of adventures to come. Of course the main advantage was that we had completed our family, provided them with life and we were still only twenty seven years old. Naturally we were pleased and so proud of our own little brood.

Pam absolutely doted on these products of our love for each other. She made them clothes, knitted them matching outfits, always bought them little presents and surprises and when they got older took them to school without fail. Once when I had my own little tribe in tow an old soldier spotted the charming trio, patted me on the back and said to me "Blimey, son you have done your bit for Great Britain." I looked at my precious boys and felt so proud, but It

wasn't me that made them what they were, but Pam's special attention that she plied on them. Her love and devotion for them was to
be repaid when they were grown up.

Chapter 11. Adventures Ahead

This life-changing increase in our family did not change our way of life. We carried on the way we had before. Of course I had to buy a much larger van, one that could take our three kids and, of course, Pam's ever-growing mobile wardrobe. Every weekend we went on expeditions, always with an imaginative reason, maybe it was to find the Lost Treasure of Epping Forest or to look for traces of Ancient Britons, Dinosaurs, Pirate's treasure, Crashed planes or anything else that we could think of. Pam would sit in the van with a newspaper and a cup of tea, her feet up on the large suit case, I vowed that one day that cumbersome article of luggage would 'accidentally' fall out of the van, but I never had the heart to upset my lovely Pam.

As our family grew we could extend the range of our expeditions, Cornwall, Devon, Dorset and of course Glorious Wales were now in reach and the equipment that Pam could not do without grew in volume.

Later that year we went to Durdle Door, a beautiful place in Dorset with a campsite on the top of some cliffs. We arrived at this lovely serene field where the silence was only broken by the screeching of the swallows and the mooing of the cows. The camping field was

almost empty so we pitched our tent in a place where we could get a good view of the clifftops and the sea beyond them. That night was very clear giving us a perfect view of the stars, even the Milky Way. Being from London we had never seen such a glorious sight before, so we laid on our backs gazing at the grand display of stars. I lay there for some time until all was quiet, Pam and all our kids had quietly drifted off to sleep, all of us cuddled up together under the brilliant stars. This was obviously a perfect spot for peace and quiet. I was so pleased to be there with my precious family.

The following day we all went to the beach and into a local market that only had a dozen or so stalls, ah, so dreamy!

The sun was beating down so we went back to our haven of solitude, a tent to you, but we couldn't believe our eyes. This huge once empty field was now absolutely crammed to capacity and as noisy as a Sunday in Petticoat Lane. There were so many scooters and vans squeezed in, and they were so close to each other that we had the choice of conversations to listen to.

It seems that all these noisy, enthusiastic, riders were just returning from 'The European Scooter Rally' and were shouting aloud in order to brag about their scooters and how far they had been and how loud the engine sounded when revved up. What's more they all had radios and record players turned up to full volume, naturally they danced the night away and clinked the empty beer bottles in rhythm to the grating music. Not fearing anything I went out of the tent and explained that we had small children inside who needed their beauty sleep but somehow the volume of their music had struck them deaf, they never even acknowledged that I was there, so the was nothing to do but turn my van radio on at full blast, " That'll show them" I said, but I don't think that they even heard my puny little radio. Pam said "Come inside now before you lose your temper and hit someone." I took one look at the heaving raucous remains of The European Scooter Rally, there were at least a thousand of them so I thought to myself "No Chance" and retreated to the safety of my bed!

The following morning the howling mob had run out of howls and were slowly and silently packing their gear away and gradually drifting away from the once most peaceful bit of Britain and were slowly kickstarting their scooters and spluttering their way back to Scooterist's Paradise

Later that morning Pam came to the rescue of our disastrous weekend break by cooking a proper Camper's fry up for breakfast on our faithful old paraffin stove. We fed our three boys and the youngest, John, guzzled his bottle and burped with contentment. With fresh bread, West Country butter, home cured bacon, and lashings of tea we were forced to lay about in the sun feeling contented and very parental. I was so very grateful for having such a special woman for my wife. The gorgeous Pam.

I held her hand and told her that I loved her, she smiled sweetly and kissed me, I was so happy!

As we continued with our nomadic weekends our boys grew bigger and bolder, the baby of the family, John, was no longer content with a bottle with a teat on it, he asked for egg sandwiches and other such lorry drivers delights. Our middle boy, Bill, would eat anything placed before him, especially sweets, cakes and in fact anything that caught his eye. The oldest boy, Glenn, by far the tallest and quietest, simply joined in with anything that was edible.

You would think that with their straight forward and simple tastes, Pam would not have any trouble catering for her growing brood but, no, Pam just had to lavish her love onto them by giving them 'special' treats. Local delicacies and specialities just had to be served to our home-bred eating machines. No Ice Cream Parlour could be passed without sampling the Knickerbocker Glories, Banana boats and Fruit cocktails. No wonder they grew so fast. Pam would never say "No" to anything that pleased them, I knew of course that her

'over the top' kindness was a product of negligence and the loveless life that she endured as a kid. She had the dignity not to talk about the needs that she and her sisters had put upon them.

Pam was nervous by nature, she never liked the lights being turned off at night and always insisted that a low glimmer be left on. This was a direct result of war time horrors, her dad was away in the Army, serving in France and Germany, I have already mentioned her mum had a passion for beer and would, when an air raid was taking place, be out in a local pub getting herself boozed up, arriving back home through the bomb damage in no state to care for her very young girls. Pam had an older sister Maureen, just three years older than her, who comforted her when the bombs were dropping. They lived very close to a huge power station that was often targeted making the night a very scary time, and if the contemptuous 'Lord Haw Haw' featured the power station in his nightly radio propaganda, this would magnify her fears and prevent her from sleeping. She sometimes spoke of the run-down block of flats and her intense fear of the rats that ran up and down the passage that only had lino on the floor. Her only comfort was a cuddle with her sister.

Yes, she was caring and indulgent to our little family, which made me be so proud of her and love her even more.

Tragedy struck when we were bringing up our family. Our second boy, Bill was only born a couple of weeks when Pam's Dad, Charlie, was involved in an industrial accident. He worked in a nearby timber yard and was loading a lorry when he fell from the top of the high load damaging his head and putting him into a coma. He was taken to the London Hospital, Whitechapel and he stayed in this coma for three months until he finally passed away. This traumatic event only made her more nervous than ever, she would not let her boys out of her sight and fussed over them day and night. Charlie was not a sight that a nervous, sensitive daughter should see, so I visited Charlie every night leaving Pam waiting outside in our van while I spoke to a silent, motionless Charlie who was gasping his last few breaths.

Chapter 12. A big decision

When Pam's Dad, Charlie, died her selfish, alcoholic Mum was left to look after and protect her two very young daughters, the three eldest sisters had married and left home, but although she promised to change her ways the beer won the battle yet again. Why did we ever think that she would be able to go without her alcoholic support and give it up for good?

The situation got worse, when her Mum was out of her brain with booze she would meet 'some bloke' in the pub and take him home for

the night. Pam's younger sisters who were just twelve and fourteen, we felt were in danger so every day Pam loaded our three young boys into the Pram and early in the morning push her precious load a couple of miles to see if the young sisters were safe. She did this every day, whatever the weather. I was working full time so felt that I was not doing enough. I spoke to her mum, threatened her, tried to bribe her but she just nodded in approval and immediately carried on with this despicable behaviour. The toll of this hard work was telling on my precious Pam. She was constantly tired, worried, irritable and certainly not the angelic woman that I married. I just could not see this special woman suffer any more so again my belief in direct action came into my mind. Shortly after yet another very upsetting confrontation I went to pick up Pam and our boys from the now bare and uncomfortable home of Pam's Mum. On arrival I found Pam in tears and the young girls huddled together for comfort. I did my best to comfort them but the boozy mum just faced me, pushing her face into mine and breathing her beer laden breath into my mouth. She started to curse me and swear at me and not surprisingly I lost my calmness and slapped the drunken trollop right round her face. Then, not knowing what I was going to do, I loaded Pam, her two young sisters, my three boys and the large pram into my van and headed for home. As soon as I got home I phoned the 'Prevention of Cruelty to Children' and spoke to an officer and off loaded my guilt to him. He warned me that taking matters in my hands, was not the best thing to do and that he would visit us the next day. As he said he arrived early the following day, when he arrived I was surprised to see him in a full dark blue uniform with badges, epaulettes, silver buttons, medals and a service cap worn at the right angle.

He warned me about slapping a woman just as Pam's boozy Mum rushed into the room shouting at the top of her voice, "

"Sir, he hit me yesterday" The officer looked at the drink raddled woman and calmly said "I don't think that anyone has been hit. Have you been drinking today?" The answer was there for all to see! I felt very guilty about what I had done to her Mum and was not sure if Pam would approve of my behaviour, but when we got home she just sidled up to me and gave me a gentle kiss.

The Officer gave me a talking to, telling me that violence solved nothing and that he would cure her of her drink problem. A few weeks later I received a phone call, it was our own Children's Officer, he simply said "That bloody woman, I feel like throttling her!" I kept quiet!

Chapter 13. On Our Own Again

At one time Pam thought that she would like to work again. She had recently passed her driving test and felt that she would love to drive for a living, so applied for a job with the Meals on Wheels service of Hackney Council. Well of course she was accepted just as long as she passed the council's own driving test.

Naturally she was a bag of nerves about taking yet another driving test and wanted to cancel the appointment. I gave her a confidence building talk which helped her but only had the effect of making me nervous. I had, when she passed her government driving test, bought her a nice little car as a congratulatory token and she loved this car and loved visiting the shopping centres in it. I pointed out to her that her own car was very much the same as the little vans used by The Meals on Wheels service and that she would sail through such a paltry little driving test, and she did!

The very next day she went to work, but not before she glamorised herself. She wore the very trendy denim jeans and denim jacket, she added a red kerchief knotted at the right angle in her neck and of course, however would she get through the day without her trade mark beads dangling about her slim and shapely body.

She returned home full of confidence and so pleased with this new job, as well as delivering the food she was told to look at the old folk and to report anything that was not well with them. Well, Pam just could not but offer friendly advice and care, so she had to stop and talk to all the sad and lonely souls and offer them sympathy along with the cottage pie and rhubarb and custard. Naturally she was nearly always late back to the depot and argued that these pour souls needed some sympathetic and understanding treatment, but she was not listened to. "That is not your job" she was often told. After a while she was taken off of this job and told that she would have to take over the deliveries to the kitchen. This involved driving a two-ton van and loading it with heavy heated canisters and taking them to some of the kitchens. The supervisor was a large muscular woman who threw these back- breaking canisters like they were as light as feathers. Little dainty Pam just could not lift them and was soon warned about her poor work effort. I told her to tell them what to do with their job and not to damage her dainty body. At that time she weighed only six and a half stone. She looked for and soon found another job!

The years flew by and now our little boys, now three of them after the birth of John, were young men, more interested in girls, loud music and having a sly drink. No matter what their age was she was still doting upon them, and even more worried about them now that they stayed out late. So worried that she would not go to bed until they were all in and safely snoring in their beds in spite of them all being full grown.

Within a short time Glenn walked in one evening and announced that he was going to move in with his girlfriend, then John followed on and bought a small flat and moved in with his girlfriend. Bill with just a hint of class decided to get married, in a registrar's office rattling the cage of the Welsh Druids once again. Before we realised it, they had all departed with not so much as a hint of ceremony. It was only then that we realised that we would be on our own for the first time, the house was morbidly silent and empty and the 'phone stopped ringing every fifteen minutes. We did not like it one little bit, but this near solitude gave us time keep our love alive and strong. But we had no need to be too lonely because eventually we would be blessed with nine grandchildren who would keep us busy and give us plenty of love.

We had kept our love of travelling and exploring alive and had long given up our tent because we bought something that we had wished for ever since we first went to Wales, a caravan. Pam was delighted and soon put her impeccable stylish touch to our home on wheels. I never got a look in, I just paid for all the luxuries, but I was happy to do so because it made her so happy.

Chapter 14. Friends and Neighbours

I never heard Pam say a bad word about anyone, she simply liked everyone whoever they were, we live in a multicultural area, and she never judged anybody by their colour, religion or culture but she would criticise some people who didn't dress 'sensibly'. " She should never wear those colours together" or "That dress is too small for her" were the worst comments that she would say about anyone. So when a young Indian couple moved in near us Pam couldn't wait to introduce herself to this tiny, pretty young woman and to compliment her on her stylish, colourful Indian clothing. From the very start these connoisseurs of style became close friends, the young woman's name is Riz and she is dainty, pretty and enchanting. Pam soon became close to her and Riz visited her regularly and admitted her fondness for Pam. Before too long a bewitched Pam told her that she would like to adopt her, but I had to point out to Pam that Riz's husband might have something to say about it. Pam's answer was "but she is so lovely". Riz is still one of our neighbours and is now the mother of five children and still talks to me about her 'almost' Mother. When Pam was suffering Riz called in to see her and to hold her hand.

Over forty years ago the house next to us was empty and we noticed that someone was opening the widows every day, being inquisitive or perhaps nosey, I took a sneaky look. Inside was a man decorating the rooms by standing on a rickety box, as well as being rickety it was much too low. Being a helpful kind of a bloke I tapped on the window, startling the would be decorator, and offered to lend him my very useful stepladder. At first he seemed reluctant to talk but soon realised that my ladder would be beneficial and accepted my offer. It seems that he and his wife and two young girls were going to be our new neighbours. They were Turkish, he spoke English, the two little girls spoke English, but Mum hardly spoke any English at all. This was not going to stop Pam from having a chat with her new neighbour. The next day I noticed that Pam was in the garden looking over the fence and trying her best to talk to the mum of the family. Her name was Zehra, but we called her Sarah and that is what she answers to. I sat in our front room with the doors wide open watching a fine piece of miming, face pulling and exaggerated movements. Hardly any words were spoken, Pam started by asking Sarah how she was. Sarah didn't quite understand but tried to tell Pam that she had pains in her leg and hip by simply holding the troubled areas and moaning, Pam then asked if Sarah had seen the doctor by just saying "Doctor?" Sarah answered by shrugging her shoulders and shaking her head. Pam asked about treatment by just saying "tablets?" No tablets said Sarah by just shaking her head again, Pam went in and came out with some painkillers that apparently was of benefit to the much relieved Sarah, and so began a forty year friendship and a helpful neighbour. Sarah still lives next to me, her husband died about five years ago, the two little girls have moved out of London and are now grandmothers, and Sarah speaks pretty good English. Now that both Sarah and I are on our own I keep an eye on her and drop in every day to see her but I just can't compete with the Turkish television that she watches endlessly.

When we were in our early forties Pam had health problems so naturally we visited the doctor. She was sent to the hospital for tests and eventually it was decided that she required a Hysterectomy. I knew that she would be frightened but strangely she took it all in her stride and before long she was admitted to St.Bart's Hospital in the City of London. Naturally she was placed in the Women's Surgical Ward. Most of the patients were older women and Pam with her loveliness and youthful looks stood out like a beacon of glamour and her smile lit up this room full of ailing ladies.

Pam had her operation and though a bit uncomfortable remained in high spirits, before long she was trotting around the ward talking to all the patients, and bringing them a bit of comfort. One of the older ladies had her leg amputated and naturally was depressed and afraid of the new life that may lay ahead. She was so uncomfortable and sad. Pam's natural charm and her ability to chat about most things soon got her talking and taking notice of what was happening in the ward. The older lady was looking just a bit bedraggled and sad so Pam offered to wash and set her hair. The attention that she was now getting made a miraculous difference to her well being and prompted her to ask Pam to make her as lovely as her new found hairdresser, so not to be a disappointment to her Pam set to make this unfortunate woman feel a bit more feminine. She washed, set and styled her hair making the older lady to ask for something to make her face look brighter and attractive. Now this challenge plunged Pam into action, diving deep into her bag of lotions, skin cares and make-up she soon had this once sad old lady smiling and admiring herself in the mirror. Not content with her work she applied a touch of lipstick to her once dried up lips, squirted a few puffs of perfume and even plucked her eyebrows. What a difference this loving attention made to how the patient felt. She smiled, for the first time, kept glancing at herself in admiration and held Pam's hand every time she passed by. The Ward Sister heaped praise upon Pam's ability and slyly asked if she could do the same for some of the other patients. Unfortunately Pam was due to be discharged within a day or two, but somehow a test showed that Pam had 'an infection' and had to remain in the ward for another week. I have never known how it was done, but then I didn't care, but Pam and her magical Make-up bag managed to get all the patients feeling a lot more glamorous and pleased with themselves. It wasn't a miracle just the magic of my very special wife and her natural charm and love of people. No wonder I loved her so much!

As soon as she was discharged from the hospital I went to book another holiday, the original date for or holiday had to be postponed to allow Pam to have her operation. But no problem, well that is what I thought, but on revisiting the very helpful Travel Agent we found that he no longer was helpful. This was now late in the summer season and the headlines in the national papers stated that there was now not one vacancy in the whole of the Mediterranean area, the once friendly and helpful agent was now surly and argumentive man. When I got on my soap box and reminded him of his obligation, he simply picked up the day's edition of a national paper and waved it under my nose, "Read that he insisted" Well there was no arguing with the headlines. Not one holiday in the Mediterranean area! So after another rant from me up on my soapbox, he reluctantly returned with an offer of a hotel room in Ibiza. We never fancied going to Ibiza because of its reputation for drugs, noise and trouble. The surly one was now even more surly and getting louder by the minute. I could see that Pam was getting uncomfortable with the argumental confrontation, so I gave in and said just a bit niggled "OK, We will take this offer "and I walked out of the office with a face like thunder. Within a few days we found ourselves at Gatwick Airport and stepping aboard a small plane, it had two seats on one side of the plane and two on the other side, it reminded me of those planes that you see in war films when they take the saboteurs to behind the enemy lines. It was cosy and when it moved we had a sensation of flying, well of course we *were* flying, we could see both wings from the seats that we occupied and when the plane banked the feeling was thrilling, I wanted to whistle the Dambusters March. Pam was silent. The flight was short and as we looked down at the Island of Ibiza it was parched and all we could see was the yellow colour of the earth. It hadn't rained for ages!

We left the little airport and a bus took us to our hotel, Pam's face was not good when she spied this downtrodden building. It was shabby and dusty and just a bit spooky, I immediately named it 'The Bates Motel', Pam was not impressed with it! The interior lived up to the impression that the exterior had given us. The rooms I will leave to your imagination, no relation to the rooms in those glossy brochures. The bed sheets were like cardboard the bed cover was closely related to the bed sheets, a bit of grimy string was used to flush the toilet and the bloody tap would not stop dripping. The whole building was tacky. After an itchy night we descended for breakfast. A hard as iron bread roll and a hard boiled egg, that was it. So we decided to walk into town to find a restaurant, the back streets were grey and in need of a good sweeping. Again I gave it a name 'Stepney with sunshine'. Within a day or so, it began to rain, It came down by the bucket load, resulting in the yellow dusty earth turning into custard coloured mud. However the copious amount of rain brought life into the parched earth and within a few days the whole island threw up large leafy plants that completely changed the whole island into a tropical hideaway. We now settled down on the beach and in the evenings we had some experimental testing of the results of the recent surgery. Ten out of ten if you must know. The mystery that explained why there was not a single holiday in the whole of the holiday capitol of Europe was explained to us as soon as we arrived in this 'Fun Centre' was simply because it was late in the year and all the good hotels and restaurants were closed for the winter! It taught us to never believe a word that you read in the Papers!

Chapter 15. Caravan of Dreams

We had been abroad quite a few times, flying to Spain and The Balearic Islands and later to Turkey but a new kind of experience lay before us now, Taking the caravan on the Ferry to France. In spite of her nervous disposition, we just set off with very little knowledge of the other side of the Channel. Of course she worried about everything, are we on the right side of the road? Have we got enough fuel? Where were we going? She had no need to worry, I coped well with driving on the wrong side of the road and my Boy Scout map reading skills were still in my head and came in handy. I had taken French at school but that was years ago and I struggled to speak to the natives, by now I was regretting not paying attention to my French master and Pam in a fit of annoyance asked me a silly question " Why didn't you concentrate on French at school? To which I replied "Well I was only twelve and I had other things on my mind". She said "What did you have on your mind at twelve years of age?" I replied sharply, "YOU!"

We were thrilled and exhilarated by France. As you may have guessed Pam was so excited by the French clothing shops and the food. She spent hours taking dresses from the rails, looking at them pronouncing that they were "Lovely" and would like to buy them, then she would look at the price label and ask me to convert the price into British pounds. After an lengthy time doing mental arithmetic my brain would be just a bit tired and asked her to buy something, then we go on with our day of sightseeing, but it was not possible to make her hurry because she simply looked at me in a special way and I was putty in her hands. She knew that I could never make her unhappy, because I loved her too much. Although she spoke no French, her delightful manner and her glamour broke down any barriers that may have existed. We were in a campsite on the banks of the Loire River, I had parked the caravan right next to the river so that we could enjoy the wildlife, between us and the river bank was a footpath and quite a few people walked by our front door, and I put a table and some chairs for us to eat our breakfast 'al fresco'. When the strollers passed us she would practice her French by greeting everyone with her well-rehearsed "Bonjour". The French people smiled sweetly and replied to her with smiles on their faces. Of course her smile was in evidence all the time. Every morning a man and his two young daughters rode along the path mounted on horses. This man was what every English woman desires in a Frenchman. He was handsome, smart and very charming and Pam looked out for him every day so she could wish him Bonjour, Invariably whenever he passed by we were sitting at a table eating breakfast and he would say "Bon Appetit" and Pam would flutter her eyelashes. I would say to her "He's nice and good looking too". She would reply in an innocent manner "I never noticed" But I would see her smile was even wider when our equestrian friend spoke to her.

Her love of people was clear, she would sometimes attempt to speak to shoppers in her London English and sometimes they would reply in French, neither of them understanding each other but her natural friendliness somehow charmed them. Often this special charm of hers would finish up with the two of them touching hands as Pam would awkwardly say "Bonjour". One morning we were walking in the grounds of an impressive chateau, admiring the flowers. It had been raining and the snails were out in force, climbing over the plants. A shabby man was holding a bag and collecting these snails, presumably to eat or to sell to a local café, she asked him what he was catching but this poor simple man was very shy so just opened his bag and showed her, "Oh" she said and the intrepid snail hunter moved on still pursuing his prey. This was not enough for Pam, she was determined to help this rather awkward looking man, so she dived into her bag and brought out a plastic bag, she always carried spare bags,' just in case'. In a short time she had a small bag of these slithery creatures and called to her fellow hunter, in a pure East London accent, "Here you are, Mate, I've got some for you" At last our straight faced fellow hunter smiled.

One area that we were stopping at was by the Atlantic Ocean and every little village or town had many sea food restaurants and Pam was very fond of 'Fruit de Mer' especially the delicious mussels. We sampled crab, langoustine, oyster and fish soup and enjoyed them all, Pam thought that I was so sophisticated because I could order them in French, but most of the more complex names I simply ordered them by pointing to their entry in the printed menu. We thoroughly enjoyed every one of these continental delicacies, I was keen to taste something new to us so I found a nice little quayside restaurant and walked in as if I was a knowledgeable gourmet. I scanned the menu and found seafood item that I had never seen before. I called the waiter and in East End French asked what this mystery dish was, his English was poorer than my French. He replied "Petite Poisson" which translates to 'little fish'. Being adventurous I ordered them, when they were served they didn't look too appetising. They were chopped into small pieces and were as black as coal. Pam looked at them with suspicion, pulling one of her 'don't like the look of those faces' I was determined to show that these strange looking objects were tasty and a French delicacy. So I took the plunge and put some of these coal black offerings straight into my mouth knowing that they might be very tasty but this time I was so wrong, they were vile and had a chalky feeling about them, not at all fishy or appetising. Pam asked me if they were nice, I stiffened my back, sat up and replied "Mmm, Different, but quite nice" She tentatively put them on a fork, sniffed them, gave them a strange look and finally gently slid one into her delicate mouth. Then her face drastically changed, her eyes squeezed shut, she wretched and then proceeded to call me all sorts of names. Outside I took my French to English translation book out and looked up this mystery word, it proved to be 'Cuttlefish', not the part that you give to little Joey but the meaty bit of this weird animal, it was jet black because of the Ink that was squirted to put off predators, well it certainly put us off.

Chapter 16. The Vogue Cleaners

When our boys were old enough, she decided to return to work. So along with her life-time friend Janice, they got a job in a Children's Home. They arrived on the first day looking like they had just stepped off the cover of a fashion magazine to do their very important jobs as cleaners. A lot of the social workers followed the latest trend casual dress, this meant in Pam's words, 'scruffy'. The guests of the care home were fascinated by Pam and Janice and they asked them all sorts of questions about their clothes, their families and even asked Pam's advice on their problems, and they had many. Pam with her maternal, caring nature and most important, her local accent, became very close to these hard done by inhabitants of the home. Although she was employed as a cleaner they would tell her of their problems, if anything worried them it was this very special woman that they turned to. If they had an appointment for the much feared dentist they would ask her to take them, the social workers were most agreeable to the request. So Pam accompanied them, calming them down and holding their hands just like the caring mum that she was, except she was not their mum. One of the girls, who suffered much abuse and had a record of bad behaviour became very close to and in awe of her. Both her and Janice loved these problem youths and they got loved in return. This maternal duo, because of their immaculate and stylish appearances became known as 'The Vogue Cleaners'.

The home decided that the children would benefit from the company of a pair of young goats. They were a novelty at first but as the lively pair matured and grew horns, they became difficult to manage, lowering their heads and charging anyone within their reach and of course throwing off that obnoxious goat smell. Can you guess who got lumbered with caring for these troublesome animals? Yes you guessed it, one half of the Vogue cleaners, My half!

Some times the lively animals would escape and a neighbour would phone the home demanding that they ought to take these 'bloody animals' away. Of course the managers of the home asked Pam to go and bring the escapees back. But as you may have guessed she wasn't pleased with this and told them that she had only just bought the latest style outfit and didn't want it reeking of 'smelly goats' so go and do it yourself! The once cute little 'kids' had become too much of a handful and the answer to the goat problem came one night when someone broke into the goat's enclosure and the smelly creatures disappeared. It was thought that the troublesome pair had finished up on 'A Persons Unknown's' barbecue. Pam said that she was sad to lose them but I had learned, over the years to tell she was telling lies. All the time that she swept and polished the Children's home in the morning she attended a school in Stoke Newington in the afternoon where she was a Craft Worker for an afterschool workshop. The young members of the workshop immediately took to her and wanted to hold her hand as she walked across the playground. They all addressed her as Miss and wanted to be Teacher's Pet, Pam was honoured. A lot of the pupils were Turkish and soon set about teaching Pam to swear in Turkish, she was a keen student.

Within a short time the Home was closed and the fashionable pair were out of work. Pam was offered another job with Social Services as a receptionist on the front desk of Social Service's main office, It was quite a prestigious job and I knew that with her good looks, smart appearance and friendly nature she would be perfect for this task, but it meant that she would have to leave her precious school and her loving pupils. The decision was a hard one to make but she decided that the receptionist's role would suit her.

She started and loved greeting people with her contagious smile, but she had not taken into account the users of this service. A large number of the claimants were in dire circumstances and were desperate for money, Pam was the first person that they came face to face with and they thought that shouting, threatening and calling her vile names would get them some much needed money, but this special woman, who I always thought was timid simply calmed them down and asked them to follow the proper procedure. Of course she did meet a few clients who didn't get the message and promised that all sorts of curses and ailments would visit her and once or twice became physically violent. In reply to these threats the council employed a security guard to keep the peace, Pam was pleased but when her private minder turned up but he was a skinny, nervous nineteen year old with a very shy nature. He watched over the reception area scrutinising all who entered in a very eager way, Pam was pleased and felt secure, that is until a particular 'client' started throwing the furniture about. She looked round for her hero but he had locked himself in the office leaving poor little Pam on the outside with the very unstable, irate money seeker. The very nervous keeper of the peace only came out of his refuge and settled down when the Police arrived.

Of course most of the clients admired this lovely example of femininity and treated Pam like the caring and delightful woman that she was, and the local dressmakers were so glad that they still had such a good customer as her.

After many years working for the council she reached her 60th Birthday and was immediately given her marching orders. Because she had worked for two departments of the council she was awarded just one part time pension, this is where the Turkish swear words came into their own. Now a disillusioned Pam said "It's time for me to put my feet up and be a lady of leisure" We had not given up our love of travelling and exploring and now progressed to a quite luxurious caravan and a very nice van to tow it with, I had even fitted the van out with hanging rails to accommodate Pam's never ending collection of classy, but impractical clothes. This was to be our time to indulge in looking again for the treasures, the lost tribes and unknown cities that we had dreamed up all those years ago. But this was not to be. On a visit to her doctor she was offered the post of Doctor's Receptionist, the doctor pleaded with her to take the job, a post that she finally accepted. She worked there for another seven years.

"The Vogue Cleaners"

Chapter 17. Holidays

Breaking The Law

In spite of her intelligence and skills she could be truly scatty. This scattiness was the cause of much laughter and disbelief from the people that knew her. Most of the time the incidents amused me, sometimes they annoyed me, but her charm and honesty always got her even more loved and simply added to her unique list of attractive qualities.

Here are a few of the scattiest of events that happened to her- by some coincidence mostly on our holidays in France. You can laugh if you want to.

We had quite a few vans and motor caravans in our time. These comfortable homes on wheels we kept as immaculate as we could. One was a good-looking Commer 5 berth motor caravan that was very easy to drive. Pam had a driving licence but had never driven such a large vehicle as this. As it was light and easy to handle I persuaded her to have a drive of it. She was just a bit nervous but the thought of getting behind the wheel of this fine-looking van intrigued her, so, with a few encouraging words and our kids saying "go on mum, have a go" and with the smoothness and comfort of the drive she overcame her trepidations and agreed to take the wheel.

We were on a motorway so I pulled into a service area and changed seats with her. I had never had the luxury of travelling in the living quarters of the van so I suggested that I could have a comfortable ride on the long bed that was built into the home bit of the van. I made sure that she was as comfortable as possible, made my way to the back of the van and put my feet up. I told her to start the engine and take it easy- and what ever happened to watch her speed!

The engine started easily and ticked over very quietly, she just put her foot on the accelerator and let out the clutch. The good old van smoothly started to move along the motorway and Pam, looking very pleased with herself, said "Oh it's so easy to drive, I like this!" I relaxed on the bed and had visions of her sharing the long drives that we had planned. I was so relaxed that my eye lids slowly drooped and I was soon in a light sleep. I was so relaxed that I was able to appreciate the quietness of our precious vehicle. More drowsiness- and then being woken by the rattling of the cups and saucers, the pots and pans, and all the rest of the contents of the kitchen cupboards of our mobile home from home. I jumped off of the bed and stuck my head into the driver's cab. I couldn't believe my eyes, the speedometer showed that we were travelling at well over eighty miles per hour. Pam sat in the driver's seat looking very pleased with herself and grinning. "Slow down!" I yelled. "Why? I'm doing all right aren't I?" "No you're not!" I shouted angrily. "This is not a sports car!" I shouted even more angrily. This is where that innocent charm came into practice. "Oops, sorry" she said through her girlish giggles. I was beaten by that little girl charm again.

Kidnapped By The Old Bill!

This story takes place, not in France but in Good old Dorset. While on another long weekend in the same Commer motorhome I got into a spot of bother. It was my fault, nothing to blame her for, but I may try!

The weather was glorious, the shimmering heat making those squiggly little optical illusions rise from the red hot rocks on the beach and even those noisy gulls were too hot to squawk or to snaffle the ice cream from your melting cornet.

We arrived at a magnificent cove that lay at the bottom of the steepest, roughest, pebble-strewn path that ran down the side of this scary, crumbly cliff. I thought twice about descending this deadly pathway but thought that if John Wayne could climb it on his horse then it was worth a go. Anyway, there was an Ice cream van down there and a couple of cars, so if they could do it then I could too. I edged forward and the frightening journey down began. I was very scared, my noisy kids were unusually silent and Pam sat in the back with her eyes shut as the van slithered on the loose rocks. Of course I wasn't scared, I was just a little bit wanting my mum. Well you will be pleased to hear that we reached the bottom without any of my crew losing their nerves, they left that to me. I found a nice space on the sea front, there were plenty of spaces as you might imagine. Pam put the kettle on and I went to the Ice Cream van and bought all of us a well-deserved, rapidly melting Vanilla Surprise!

After exploring the rugged cove and studying that scary looking, crumbly path, I packed my precious family into the van and with determination attempted to climb back to the top of the cliff, but I over-estimated the ability of our overloaded campervan. The first try at a climbing to the top was not good, the engine revved away but not one inch of progress was achieved. After a few more tries we were still in the same place, our kids thought it was a lot of fun but I was getting more and more agitated. Just then a big bloke in a powerful car offered to tow us up the dreaded hill, but nothing seemed to be happening. So I had the bright idea of all of us getting out of the van and letting Pam get behind the wheel, but I hadn't thought it through properly. Me and our unruly mob dismounted from our van with the idea of pushing it, just to start off the ascent of the scary hill. Pam looked good behind the wheel and was obviously enjoying the little adventure, it may have been because the helpful bloke in the car was a fine example of manhood with a lovely smile that he flashed at Pam all the time. Then, suddenly and without warning, the gallant helper started to tow our van with me and my boys pushing as hard as we could. The wheels began to grip and my precious van, along with my even more precious Pam, moved at speed up the very steep and frightening hill. At this stage the plan was for all of us to jump into the back of the van and enjoy the bumpy journey to the top, but perhaps I hadn't told the handsome bloke what was in my mind because our lovely van was last seen going at a rate of knots bumpily into the unknown. I was close to a nervous calamity and urged my 'merry men' to chase this possible kidnapper and overpower him, but my small gang of reluctant volunteers were helpless with laughter and my precious wife was nowhere to be seen. I left my very unsympathetic henchmen and ran up the hill, it was steeper and longer than I thought but I eventually reached the top and found my van with Pam still behind the wheel and our rescuer with his head inside the window chatting and laughing with my precious wife, what's more she was laughing along with this 'modern highwayman' and enjoying it very much. I was not pleased at all but when he said that he was a policeman on holiday I begrudgingly thanked him.

Just then my rag-taggle band of knackered kids arrived at the top, I pushed them into the back of the van and sped off, the normally very nervous Pam said "That was fun!"

Look Where You Are Going!

Back now in France. After a long drive from the ferry we arrived in the lovely town of Blois and found a very agreeable spot on a campsite and started to prepare the caravan, but first I had to position the van properly. I needed to reverse the van and caravan, an easy job for a seasoned traveller such as me. Pam was flittering about, so I asked her to watch me go back and tell me to stop if I got too close to anything. I had shown her many times just what to do, simply stand where I could see her and tell me to stop should I get too close to anything. "Whatever you do, keep me in your sight and don't stand behind the caravan because I won't be able to see you" I emphasised. "I know, I'm not stupid" she said – and immediately disappeared behind the caravan completely out of my sight. Exasperation made me start to reverse very slowly knowing that she would simply step out of the way. Then I saw many people run towards the back of the van all waving their arms and shouting at me in French. For one moment I thought that she might be laying on the ground with a tyre mark over her belly, but no, she had walked backwards and stepped down a rabbit hole causing her to land on her bum. I ran to her and said "Why didn't you keep in sight of me?" I demanded, "I did wave to you", she said, "but you were out of my sight", I barked at her, "so I couldn't see you waving!" She thought for a second, said "Oh Yeah", and giggled.

Sweet Dreams In Calais.

Simply to get a little bit more time on holiday, sometimes we would get the late-night ferry from Calais, have a rest on the quayside and start again at dawn, quite a few campers did the same. We arrived at Dover and boarded the ferry near to midnight, the crossing was only about one hour in length, so we would have a breakfast on the ferry just as it set sail. No sooner had we finished our meal when the order to disembark was given. We drove the van and the caravan down the ramp and onto the dockside, I always loved this part of the journey because in my mind I was a kid again thinking that we were part of a huge invasion. The many cars, lorries and caravans rumbling down the ramp gave me a feeling of adventure, but it was now about half past one in the morning, too late for adventures, so we joined the couple of dozen caravans parked together in a car park where our fellow adventures had the same idea as us, to have a couple of hours sleep and then press on to the AutoRoute to the south.

We felt so secure in amongst our British companions and without even undressing we lay on the bed and soon hoped for a peaceful sleep. As usual Pam said "I will never go to sleep here" but nevertheless we both passed quickly into the 'Land of Nod' feeling pleased with ourselves.

In what seemed like just an hour later I awoke and pulled the curtain to see our part-time neighbours. But they were all gone! The sun was high in the sky and was blazing down on our mobile bedroom. I looked at the time, it was nearing midday. There was no point in rushing now so I made a cup of tea and some toast and woke my own Sleeping Beauty. "What time is it ?" she asked. "Time to go" I said and told her the time. She immediately went into a panic but the tea and toast helped to calm her down, when she was wide awake she looked out of the window and said "where is everyone?" "There they are", I said, pointing to the very suspicious dozen or so men creeping along a ditch. "Who are they?" she asked suspiciously. "They are just Illegal Immigrants looking for a lift" I replied. She swallowed the remains of her tea in one gulp and quickly clambered into the driver's cab of the van and we swiftly drove out of the huge dockyard. We picked up the AutoRoute and she sat in the cosy seat still trying to forget the supposed threat of the Immigrants and within ten minutes she was asleep. I let her have her sleep for the next hundred miles. When she eventually came to she asked "Where are we?"

French Tea Leaves

We visited most parts of France, each area has its own memory for us. This tale takes place in Brittany, in a lovely area called 'La Cote Sauvage'- in English 'The Wild Coast'. An apt name for the adventure that befell us there. This area is just a bit like Cornwall, a bit remote but beautiful and tranquil. There were not many people about so we pulled up by a pebble beach that afforded us a lovely view of the coast, the boats, and to the south you could see a far-off town. There were just a few sunbathers struggling to get comfortable on the hard and lumpy pebbles. Of course we had left the caravan on a campsite, but the back of our Transit van carried Pam's comfortable cushions and blankets that she wasted no time in laying out on the beach.

Of course she had her handbag over her arm so I told her to lock it in the van, but she dithered so I took her bag and put it under the passenger seat, shoved a heavy tool box in front of it and locked the door. "Right, that is safe!" I said knowing that no one would find it, anyway there were only a few drowsy sunbathers about and we had set up our beach bed just a few feet from our van. You won't be surprised to know that the lovely Pam soon had her eyes shut, I never went far away, just a few feet in search of seashells. Pam was restless and asked me to get her bag for her, so I went into the van, removed the toolbox to reveal a gaping space where her bag used to be. The doors were still locked and no signs of damage, but Pam was upset and close to tears, "my money, my passport, the ferry tickets and our insurance certificate were in there". Now I was upset.

We speedily left the beach and searched for a police station, when we eventually found one It looked like a scene from a desert film. The tiny shack-like building was bedded into the sand and surrounded by a barbed wire fence, it was not very welcoming. A French tricolour fluttered above the door, we rang the bell a few times and out came a plump gendarme who spoke not one word of English. He herded us into the reception where I struggled with my very poor French to explain our predicament, eventually he had an idea of what I was talking about and went to get his companion, who was young, very charming and had perfect English. His gendarme's uniform was immaculate and his teeth sparkled. Pam now had someone to listen to her tale of woe and she told it in every detail, smiling at the local bobby (I can't say that in French) and feeling good. When he had taken down all our particulars, he gave us a receipt and told us to carry on with our holiday.

We phoned Pam's bank, her credit card bank, the British Embassy and the Ferry Company to be sure that we could get back into our precious England. None of them seemed worried, so why should we.

We still had another two weeks holiday to come so we enjoyed the French countryside and food. Then came the day to return to the land of our birth. was I was nervous about arriving back in blighty with no paperwork. At this particular time there was yet another scare about illegal immigrants, people smuggling contraband and drugs. Of course I, heavily bearded and driving a Transit, knew that the custom officers would pull me and question me with rubber hoses. But first we had to show our passports and travel documents. The officer leaned on the counter and said "Passports please. "I just said "We haven't got any, they have been stolen". The calm and collected officer said "Oh. That's a shame. I hope it didn't spoil your holiday. Go on through".

Then we arrived at the customs desk. "Anything to declare?" he asked. By now I was not at all bothered. "Nothing at all!" "Go on through then." At last we were home and dry! We triumphantly boarded the ferry and I had that schoolboy fantasy of returning home after a victory. This return journey was from Caen to Poole, a much longer and relaxing journey so, when we disembarked onto this green and pleasant land, I had no fear of the petty officials that could make our lives miserable. I, quite full of self-belief, drove to the ticket inspector and flashed the replacement ferry tickets. He scanned the ticket and very wisely said "But it's all in French!" Then we drove to the Customs Officer, "Have you anything to declare?" I replied, "Yes, it's good to be home!" He rolled his eyes and waved us through.

There is a happy ending to this story, a few weeks later I received a 'phone call from France, someone had found Pam's hand bag, it had been abandoned in a nearby bush complete with all its contents, except for the cash of course. The local Mairie parcelled it and sent it back to a highly delighted Pam! Vive la France!

Parlez Vous?

Wherever we went in the world Pam strangely felt the urge to seek medical advice. She was not a hypochondriac, she just had a first class degree in worrying. Anything from sunburn after sitting for hours in the blazing sun, gnat bites, headache, belly-ache, back-ache and any little itch, twitch or scratch would make her think that her 'poor health' needed medical assistance. None of these complaints required the calling of a helicopter but Pam insisted on 'treatment' of some kind. Once in Brittany she sought the aid of a Dutch faith healer who laid hands on her stiff back. The healer was a fellow camper and a fervent Elvis fan, who sang some of "The King's" greatest hits, completely out of tune, all through the questionable treatment. At least she spoke English. In our search for treatment we visited many village pharmacies and health shops, none of whom had a clue what we were speaking about, and vice versa. I remember one small and ancient apothecary where I was served by a young woman who just stood staring over my shoulder when I spoke to her, It seemed that there was an invisible being behind me.

I had a brief knowledge of French, I could ask for tea, coffee, and simple things like that, but the technical words used by doctors and chemists went right over my very English head. I was able to manage 'Le plume de ma tante' but anything else was double Dutch to me.

We spent two weeks with my son and his family in Turkey, the sun shone every day, the food was copious and delicious but poor old Pam was not at her best. We called the hotel doctor who called on us in a minibus and took us to his surgery. This surgery, only a few yards from the hotel was in a one-roomed shop. We were asked to sit and wait in the communal one and only space with a few other patients. To be fair there was a colourful curtain separating the examination bed and the patients from the gaze of our fellow sufferers. There was a man who had a nasty cut on his hand, a woman who just lay on another bed not showing one sign of life, and a little boy who was crying - for what we never knew. Soon the charming doctor turned his attention on to Pam. She was feeling tired and dizzy so Doctor took her blood pressure. It was sky-high, alarming Pam even more. We were to fly home the following morning and Doctor Charming said that the airline would not let us fly until her blood pressure fell to an acceptable level. He put her on a drip-fed medication which lowered her pressure just a bit and then his assistant drove us back to the hotel and called on us every hour throughout the night, checking Pam's blood pressure every time. During a nail-biting night, finally the pressure dropped to a respectable level and we all flew back to England with Pam looking wonderfully fit and healthy. Everyone who saw her tanned skin and her special glow remarked how good and healthy she looked. I told her not to talk about her trouble, but as usual she ignored me and relayed the drama in blood-curdling detail.

I Want To Go Home!

Once we planned a thrilling adventure that was more thrilling than what we intended. At that time we had a very stylish vintage caravan, much admired by many people, in fact if anyone showed an interest in it Pam could very easily be persuaded to give them a conducted tour of her pride and joy.

I never planned a route or destination for our explorations of the wonderful country of France, I just headed in the right direction in hope of being delighted with what we discovered. We were seldom disappointed and having no preconceived idea of what we could find was a big part of our adventurous holidays. This particular holiday we were simply headed for 'The South of France' in expectation of the glamour and delight of the Mediterranean area. We drove off the ferry at Calais and straight onto the Autoroute that ran due south. We had been driving for some time when we came across an interesting town that was sat on top of the only hill in this otherwise flat area, a magnificent cathedral sat on the top of this hill, the town of Laon nestled around. It was tempting so I suggested that we spend the night there and set off in the morning, however the charm of this hilltop settlement persuaded us to stop just a little bit longer. On the way back up the hill to the campsite we heard an unfamiliar noise coming from the engine. A drive belt had broken so I limped the short distance to the campsite and called the local breakdown service thinking that a mechanic would simple put on a new belt and we would carry on due south. But this simple plan was not to be, the breakdown van towed our van to the local Peugeot dealer, our van was taken into the workshop and we were left standing in the very grand reception area being spoken to in French by a young, smart man called Freddy (pronounced Fredeee!) He told me to return in a couple of days to see what the repair would be. When I returned our van was nowhere to be seen and Freddy was being belligerent. To cut a long and complicated story of broken promises and lies I found that this grand and palatial workshop had farmed out the job to a small and scruffy one about 10 miles away, and we were not allowed to visit it. Never being one to take things lying down I immediately visited the secret workshop accompanied by a fellow camper who was small, bouncy and French and looked angry at the drop of a hat. He spoke no English and my French needed repairing, between the two of us we must have looked a force to beware of. The main problem it seemed was that we had arrived in the holiday week when lots of French businesses closed and they could

62

not get the parts. We had been stuck on our campsite for nearly two weeks and Pam was getting worried about getting back. I asked the bloke in the scruffy garage how much the repair would cost when it eventually got done, he quoted some sky-high amount, thinking that I was a mug. So I phoned one of my Turkish friends in Hackney who quoted a figure that was just a fraction of the French quote. As I was covered for recovery by my insurance, I called a local recovery company to recover me, my van and caravan to Calais.

PART TWO. Within fifteen minutes the recovery truck arrived to whisk us back home. If we were expecting the latest model of truck, highly-polished and decorated with chrome, then we were quite disappointed. A scruffy, greasy truck that looked like it had come straight from the breaker's yard pulled into the campsite. Out of the filthy cab stepped a French cousin of Steptoe. He was covered in greasy clothes, overweight and had a very ashy and pungent ciga-

rette dangling from his mouth. I told him that my caravan was an antique so please take care of it. He stared at our pride and joy as if I was telling lies, he was not impressed by our palace on wheels. He mounted the towing van onto the back of the recovery truck and the hooked up our caravan to the tow bar, leaving big greasy hand prints all over the front of our highly polished treasure. Once again I reminded him to take good care of our beloved caravan, he replied "Oui, Oui" and immediately crashed it down from the pavement.

This is where Pam comes into the story, as usual she was immaculately dressed and seeing as we were about to take a sea journey she was dressed from head to toe in nautical white. A brilliant white blouse matched her snow-white trousers and white wedge shoes. She took one look inside the cab and her face fell, well more than fell, it grimaced. Our driver could see the horror on Pam's face and apologised, "Pardon Madam" he said about three times and searching down the back of his seat produced yesterday's newspaper that was just a shade cleaner than the greasy seat. Pam smiled sweetly at him and he relaxed a bit. Then off we went on the road to Calais which was about one hundred and forty miles away, home was getting nearer!

The day was hot and sticky, the cab of the truck was losing its battle with the air-conditioning unit but soon the driver called into a service station to refuel,

I took this break to wander into the shop for something to ease our dry throats , I soon found some large, bright orange, sticky ice lollies and bought three- one for Pam, one for me and of course one for our driver. Ever cautious Pam had a tea towel that she spread over her lap and I tried to be as careful as I could be, but Monsieur Le Chauffeur could not control his thirst and slooped and sucked his lolly dropping most of it down on to his greasy T-shirt and spreading the rest around his chin. Pam got a fit of the giggles, and so did the driver.

By now we were getting near Calais and our driver was looking a bit tired and uncomfortable, he was rubbing his chest, holding the steering wheel with one hand and trying to search through his overflowing glove department with the other, unaware the truck was veering from left to right in a very frightening way. Then a big smile crossed his face. "Voila!" he said, as he held up a plastic pill bottle, then struggled to unscrew the top of the bottle and then....tipped out three tablets into the palm of his greasy, sweaty hand. Pam remained silent as she sat next to him waiting for the crash.

She looked at our heroic driver and gently asked him about his action with the tablets. He patted his chest and with a worried look upon his face said "C'est mon Coeur" – "It's my heart". Pam said "Ooooooh".

We all stayed silent until we reached Calais.

Chapter 18. Cousin Arthur

I had a cousin, Florrie, who with her husband, Arthur, lived just across the road from us. They were both older than both Pam and me. Florrie was another stylish dresser and was kindness itself to us and our boys, tragically dear Florrie died suddenly at the age of eighty, leaving Arthur alone to care for himself. Arthur was a bit older than Florrie and was devastated and not having to look after himself before was rather overwhelmed and very lonely. He had the company of another of my cousins, Arty, he was of course Florrie's brother. Within about a year Arty passed away leaving poor old Arthur all on his own. Both me and Pam watched over Arthur, Pam and another relation would do his shopping, tidy up and I would go to buy Arthur a pack of cans of beer that he shared with close neighbours. Our other relative soon moved up country but nothing to worry about, both me and Pam carried on caring for Arthur.

Arthur did not have much experience of cooking so Pam gave him lessons and handy tips, and when he needed to he 'phoned her and she guided him. I could hear them both laughing and sometimes shouting at each other in an effort to further educate Arthur in the rules of the kitchen. Sometimes Pam would put the 'phone down

Pam and her sisters

and walk to Arthur's flat and give him face to face lessons, when they would end up laughing and calling one another names. Arthur loved Pam and these lessons and soon was able to cook his food himself. I once called in on him when he was eating his dinner and was so surprised to see the huge dinner that he had cooked for himself. Arthur was a small and fragile man but this meal would have been a problem for Desperate Dan himself.

Pam never complained about her duties for Arthur, she enjoyed being with the now ancient Arthur, buying him treats and having fun together.

Then tragically Arthur suffered a severe stroke and was taken to Homerton Hospital, where he stayed for some months. Strangely Arthur liked being in hospital despite being even more handicapped than before. He was, in spite of everything, a jolly and convivial man and loved being with people. He was now in the company of people all day long, he made friends with the family of the patient in the next bed to him, they were a Jamaican family who fell for the now damaged charm of our Arthur. Gifts were exchanged and Arthur was always grateful and pleased to have found people who were like family to him. Of course Pam got close to this charming family and there was sadness when Arthur's time came to move to a care home.

This home was large and busy, but our fun-loving Arthur was placed in a room of his own and this didn't please him, he missed all the hustle and bustle of the busy hospital and the friends that he had made there. He stayed in this home for about two years and Pam visited him at least twice a week, always with his favourite treats, but the stroke had damaged his taste buds so it was difficult for hi to enjoy his food, Pam would hand-feed him and try to persuade him to eat well without success. She bought him skin creams, moisturisers, shampoos and even nice scented bottles to make him feel more at ease. She washed him, shaved him, cut his hair, cut his toenails and spoke tenderly to him, she was so loving to this now bundle of bones, she held his hand whenever she sat with him but in spite of this loving care from our beautiful Pam, dear old Arthur left us one wet and chilly night. He was ninety-one.

My special caring Pam never once failed to give Arthur her love and attention.

Chapter 19. Back in the old routine

Pam was now trying her best to settled down to her new job in her own doctor's surgery, but it was not so suitable for a very particular woman like her.

The surgery that Pam was very familiar with was not at all comfortable or tidy,

it was dark and gloomy and had a strong feeling of Queen Victoria about it. It had none of the latest electronic gadgets to aid the services that were on offer. The building was on three storeys plus a creepy, damp cellar, so that it meant continuously running up and down the narrow, steep staircases.

There were no facilities such as lockers for the workers clothes, just an ancient electric kettle, but the doctor would brag about his antique furniture. Of course the furniture was just worn out, out of date rubbish that never got cleaned, it was not an asset to the medical surgery. Pam complained about the rubbish but the doctor remained adamant that the surgery was beautiful. The doctor's wife was the practice manager but not at all friendly or happy and what's more not a touch of the friendly style that Pam had, and without a doubt no skill with keeping the patients happy. In fact most of them asked for Pam when they entered and when Reps visited the surgery they assumed that the attractive, smart and amiable person behind the desk was the practice manager. This assumption gave the real practice manager a very sizeable fit of anger and I guess, an attack of jealousy.

The doctor and his wife were very comfortably off Asians with a large house and servants in India but were very careful with their money and she had a large circle of friends in England who on regular occasions held 'Afternoon Tea' in each other's houses. One day the manager told Pam, who always looked nice, that she could come to the doctor's house for the next week's bunfight, Pam was flattered, Then 'madam' said "You can serve tea to all my friends". I think that you could guess just what the reply to this patronising request was. At last my kind and vulnerable wife had stood up for herself.

I have no need to tell you that the many patients simply loved her and praised her and nearly all the old men were captivated by her kind and loving nature. She had contact with them through a small serving hatch that had a sliding door, this sliding door was in a bad way from the constant slamming of it by previous staff. No such bad behaviour from Pam, when she handed out the prescriptions through the hatch a lot of the more ancient male patients would stroke her hand and she always understood that they were lonely and gave them one of her special smiles. They often went away clutching the prescriptions with a smile on their face. She was kind and affectionate to all the clientele of the surgery.

One fateful day the police came to the premises asking questions and looking about the offices, the outcome of this investigation was that the highly respected doctor was arrested and the very long established practice was closed down. Pam of course was upset but realised that we were both rather 'Mature' and did what she should have done seven years previously. She accepted that it was time to retire.

Her fan club of admiring patients presented her with flowers, chocolates and 'Farewell' cards, hugs and kisses, and one or two tears flowed.

The following another day I went with her to the now closed surgery, I have no idea why she wanted to visit it, but she stood outside the lifeless building and for once was quiet. Then an old Greek lady arrived and held her hand while she said a prayer in Greek, then another lady pressed a little gift into her hand and simply said "Thank you!" A couple of shopkeepers banged on the windows and gave her a wave and smiled at her and three Indian builders stood on their scaffolding and waved to her, more unscheduled meetings with her ex-clients, and more cards and thanks from her friends. I remember thinking that I was not the only one to think that she was special, but the good wishes and tributes were yet to finish. We went into the local pharmacy, a place where she was loved and admired, she was presented with a large bottle of perfume, just the sort that she preferred, more hugs and kisses and thanks and we were off home to peace and quiet. Pam looked uneasy when she realised that her busy work life had finished so I promised her more adventurous holidays.

We were both approaching the dreaded age of seventy so perhaps it was time to concentrate on rest and leisure, after all we had worked for it for many years. However I couldn't bear the thought of kicking my heels about all day so I promised to do the odd job that might come in, no more knocking on doors for work. I was a keen gardener so I was able to do as I pleased and when we wanted we could go shopping, her favourite hobby, I wasn't too keen but when she poked and prodded her way around dress shops she was so happy and I could wander about until she had taken every item of clothing from the rail, scrutinise it, pulled a face and say "No it's not what I like" Our Daughter-in- Law, Joanne would often aid and abet her to do a bit of afternoon bargain hunting, and the pair of the best critics of style and glamour could easily spend a few hours driving the shop assistants mad with their incessant questions.

This routine carried on happily for a good few years, both Joanne and Pam congratulating themselves on the bargains that they had, but like as not within a day or two the bargains lost their appeal and were unceremoniously carted back to the store for Pam and Joanne to claim their money back.

We still went on caravan trips, but now our adventurous yearnings had waned so The New Forest and even Dover were adventure enough for us. Eventually we decided to finish with our wandering passions and to set our little mobile love nest up on a camp site in Hertfordshire and roam no more. This was so right for us, the site was right in the middle of 'The Bargain Hunter's Triangle', with all the designer clothes centres just a few miles from us whichever direction you took. Joanne and Pam, the champion shoppers, were delighted!

Life was good now, we were about seventy years old, Pam, just like fine wine had matured, she was still as beautiful as ever, her glowing complexion showed up her smooth, wrinkle free skin, her smile was just as alluring and I loved her even more. We were now spending all our time together and I for one was enjoying it very much. I had often thought that I could not settle down to doing nothing all day, but having Pam stay by my side was thrilling. I was just as much infatuated by her as I was all those many years ago, and I just loved walking out together showing off my beloved wife. We were enjoying the luxury of lying in bed later in the morning, that is until Pam's strong addiction to her morning tea had her twisting me around her little finger, making me get up out of our cosy bed and making her breakfast and presenting it to her on a tray. I pride myself in having made breakfast in bed for her every day since we got married. After breakfast she read the papers and spent a couple of hours on the 'phone chatting away about nothing in particular to Joanne, her sisters, her friends, in fact anyone she wanted to. After all we were well and truly retired and Pam took full advantage of it. I paid more attention to my garden, pottered about, chatted to the many men of my age that I met on my morning meanders around the area and generally just enjoyed life. We both were living the life of Riley!

Most weekends we stopped at our caravan, again not doing anything in particular except chatting, drinking tea and of course looking around the women's clothing shops. Life was so pleasing! Our boys and their numerous kids would visit us at the caravan and Pam, in order to be Nan of the year, made a Sunday afternoon tea for them. Plenty of scrumptious food, lots of tit-bits all served up with fancy paper tissues and a small bunch of flowers on the table. She was so particular about stylish presentation, I was so proud of her! Before they went home the grandchildren always got some pocket money and a loving kiss.

Chapter 20. The Queen of Hearts

For many years I had the job of visiting clubs, homes and other such venues to entertain the members. I always, if possible, booked the same pianist to accompany our, somewhat happy go lucky show. I had used my mate Laurence Payne for donkey's years, but a contract had made him not available. I just had to find a new pianist, well I found one but I can't for the life of me remember where. Our new Musical Director was Michael Topping, known simply as Topping. He was an over the top Queen and never cared who knew he was gay. Pam would often come to these gigs and as soon as she saw Topping I'm afraid it was love at first sight. He was bold, loving and full of fun and just a bit naughty. He would laugh at anything, and Pam absolutely loved him. They would chatter about anything and laugh all the way through their conversations. We would drive to the venues in one car and me being the driver I was forgotten as this Chalk and Cheese couple giggled and became suggestive all the way to our destination.

He had a fine voice and could sing anything from Ave Maria to Knees up Mother Brown, with rude words inserted of course. He had an outrageous laugh that would start the audience off, and start him off as well. Once when we were playing to a room full of ancient members of a care home, a very old lady, who was sitting in the front row had an urge to scratch herself in a rather delicate part of her body. Topping never spotted this but Pam made sure that he would not miss this spectacle, he laughed so much that he fell off of the piano stool and sat on the floor braying like a love-sick donkey. Of course Pam had to leave the room. When we all went on these trips, sometimes great distances, I, along with Pam would pick Topping up from the station and Pam would always give him a small gift that she had bought especially for him, it was always some tasty tit-bit. Sometimes a fresh fruit, sometimes a tasty cake, but his favourite was a small tub of Houmous, his eyes would light up at the thought of this tasty treat. He would sit in the back of the car slapping his lips and almost purring with delight and Pam would fuss over him like a mother hen and ask "Was that nice?". Of course the answer was always reply "Mmmmmm" When, after the performance was over, we dropped Topping off at the station. He would bid us both goodbye with the loudest, campest air-kiss always accompanied by an over- the-top "Mwaaaaaaah!"

Now that we were in our less active age, we would spend every weekend in our bucolic retreat, doing nothing much, just being together and enjoying each others company.

Chapter 21. The End of a Dream

This was the start of the worst time I our lives. I distinctly recall that it was the week after the August Bank Holiday. The previous week, the campsite was overflowing with campers, but this weekend not many people had arrived, only a few of us more hardened caravaners. The weather was fine and we visited the nearby small town of Hertford, Pam strolled around the shops, we had coffee and cakes, still nothing out of the ordinary until it was time to go to bed. It was midnight, I was in bed first and Pam was still primping and preening the caravan, she pulled the curtains shut about three times, rearranged the toilet items that were around the washing basin and stared at herself in the mirror very intently. I lay in bed getting more and more agitated and finally said "What are you doing over there? Come to bed, it's getting late" She turned to me and simply said "I've just been down to the cellar, did you know that we had a cellar?" A thought that she may be ill ran through my head leaving me breathless and agitated, I didn't know how to answer this strange question. She went on saying "The cellar is big, in fact there are two of them. They must have been your Nan's" My Nan died in 1940 when both of us were just two years old so this strange statement sent a strong chill down my spine, now I was scared! I asked her to come to bed again. "I'm not ready yet, Anyway, where are we?" I looked around to make sure and replied "In our Caravan"

"This is our caravan?" she asked, I was now beginning to shake and I pinched myself to make sure that I was awake. She looked around her much loved weekend retreat and said "But it's horrible, who made it? Was it you?" My heart began to thump and my head spun. Again, I pleaded with her to come to bed. "I will if you get all those kids out of our bed" Somehow I persuaded her to join me In bed, I cuddled her but it didn't feel like my loving Pam. Within minutes she was fast asleep, but I was so worried that I could not sleep, I just lay awake watching her, it was probably the longest night of my life. She woke up early and I was watching every move that she made. "How do you feel today?" "I'm alright, why are you asking?"

I didn't know if I should tell her of the strange happening, well I did and she almost laughed, "Are you sure? I can't remember anything like that." She said.

I made her a cup of tea and started to pack, "Why are you getting ready to go home?" she asked, I told her some Cock and Bull story and we went home. We had dinner and she seemed absolutely normal. "Perhaps I misunderstood the situation." I told myself and tried my hardest to put the whole incident out of my mind, but it kept me on edge all day.

The following day, being Monday, I took her to her doctor and relayed the strange story, she just sat in the Surgery not saying a word. The doctor who we didn't know, asked her a few questions and opened a drawer and took out a folder. It contained a lot of questions which he asked the bewildered Pam. As usual she looked so well and stylishly dressed, and it seemed that she was enjoying the quiz game that the doctor was playing. He asked her what her name and address was. She rattled of her particulars and looked very pleased with herself, that was until the next question." What day is it today?" asked the doctor, Pam offered three answers but none of them was correct. Doctor then asked her what the date was, where we were and why she was there, she failed all questions. However when he asked her who the Queen was her face lit up and she answered "Lizzy", not very respectful but absolutely correct. The next set of questions were very tricky and even I was a bit confused. He read her an address and told her to remember it, she couldn't. He asked her to spell words, she couldn't, he asked her to spell some words backwards, she couldn't, neither could I. By now she was so disappointed that her face looked so sad. I felt tears run down my cheeks because I realised that my promise to take care of her, that I made all those year ago was not going to be kept.

The doctor sat at his desk and summed up his findings on the examination in straight forward words, no evading the truth now, "My opinion is, taken in view of the results, is that you most likely have Alzheimer's disease. Take this letter to the Alzheimer's Clinic for their opinion"

We bid the doctor goodbye and thanked him, but thanked him for what? This was probably the worst news that we had ever received!

We left the surgery in silence and I held her hand as we crossed the busy road, on the other side of the road Pam broke the silence, "Trust me to get such a bloody illness" For some unknown reason we both laughed. As we carried on she was strangely distant and I was close to tears.

When we arrived home I asked her if she wanted a cup of tea, she said yes, and then offered to make it, I agreed and left her to her own devices to make the welcome 'cuppa'. I heard her rattling the cups and saucers and in she came with two steaming cups. I said "Thanks" and looked into the cups, we had two cups of boiling water, no tea bags, just clear boiling water. I took a deep breath and tried to gather my jumbled thoughts. I simply stood by her not knowing what to do. Then it became clear, I immediately phoned Jo-anne who told me to calm down and wait for her to come over. Pam simply waited for our reinforcements to arrive looking calm and of course looking healthy and attractive. We decided to 'phone the Alzheimer's clinic, eventually I spoke to a specialist doctor who listened to my story and heard that I was so worried about my wife. She told me to visit the clinic the next day. She asked me for the usual particulars including her age, I immediately went on the defensive, I said "Well, she is Seventy Nine, but don't think that she is a little old lady, she is beautiful and clever" completely forgetting that she recently could not make a cup of tea. "Don't worry we will look after her, come down tomorrow in the afternoon and I will see her" The next day we arrived at the clinic and sat in the foyer. After ten minutes the door opened and the doctor called to the dozen or so elderly patients, "Mrs Walker?", Pam stood up and I noted the doctor casting her eye over Pam who was wearing a very stylish red coat, smart high heels, immaculate hair and one of her famous smiles on her lovely face. Doctor looked at me and said "Mmmm" They went into the large examination room where doctor asked her more questions that went right over her head. Pam continued to smile looking as cool as a cucumber and not at all flustered.

Doctor then asked Pam to walk around the large room, she leapt to her feet, still giving us her glamour routine and paraded around the room as if she was on a catwalk, twirling her coat whenever she turned. She seemed to be enjoying this game of fashion modelling! The doctor and her assistant mumbled between them and the specialist doctor confirmed that she was indeed suffering from the dreaded disease, and for us to return next week.

In my dreamlike state I thought that she would give us some tablets that would cure her, but that was not to be!

The following week we visited the clinic to be told about the illness, and what we should do and gave us a small pack of pills for Pam to take starting that night, she explained that one of these medications would dampen down the effects of Alzheimer's disease, but this was not a cure. So far nobody had mentioned the fact that she would die, of course we all knew but never wanted to think about such a tragic result. I foolishly thought that if ignored it, it would just go away. It was clearly a case of wishful thinking on my part. Then a trainee adviser spoke to me, mentioning that I should prepare myself for a very difficult 'journey' that would eventually finish with her death. My stomach turned over and I felt fear like I had never known before. Why did he have to tell me such tragic news in such a calm and collected manner? Why did he have to tell me at all? I felt like shaking him, but of course it was not his fault, I just felt numb and wanted to blame someone and he just happened to be the one who stood before me! What should I do? What should I say to our family? How will I cope with such a disaster? I was suddenly in a much different world than I had been before

At this crucial stage I decided to get rid of our much loved caravan knowing that I would get an objection and disappointment from Pam, but she just accepted the situation without any comment, this lack of reaction was not at all like Pam and confirmed to me the extent of her illness.

From that moment on I took over all household duties, never letting her lift a finger, she said that she was bored and wanted to help but I stood firm, but then the stark truth hit me like a ton of bricks. She was not going to come out of this alive, although we had been warned of this, I simply refused to believe it. Why would such a lovely, warm, and loving person like her be

made to suffer? After arguing with myself and dreaming of a treatment being found to cure her, I, at last realised that this was a very serious situation and threw aside my fantasies o f miraculous cures and broke down in tears. If I looked at her I would sob, I told a few people and sobbed even more, I even stopped strangers in the street and poured my heart and tears out to them. This was getting to be a burden, but somehow I got some morbid satisfaction out of this tragic behaviour, I knew it was not good but I could not stop it. Even Pam herself told me to get a grip of myself, but this was the greatest tragedy that had ever struck the pair of us, so why shouldn't I? I just could not accept the truth! Then the help and advice trickled in, most people when told would say "If there is anything that I can do to help you, just ask" but they didn't mean it, or they would say that their mum or dad or gran had the dreaded disease and that was 'terrible' and relayed in all it's gruesome detail just how much their beloved relatives had suffered. This was not what I wanted to hear and just the mention of it made my tears flow again. Eventually I just told the offending, thoughtless individuals not to tell me such horror tales.

But a return visit to the Alzheimer's Clinic was a different matter, I was handed lots of leaflets and booklets that just simply overloaded my aching brain, I could not take in so much information and this made me feel useless. Then I was introduced to Carol, an adviser and an employee of the clinic, who would come to be a friend and a source of comfort to us. Carol was a straight talking, kind, helpful person. She had a soothing tone to her speech and an understanding nature. She visited us and immediately mentioned how smart that Pam looked and Pam told Carol where she had bought these clothes and how much they were. Pam was at that time fully mobile so she took Carol upstairs and showed her almost every item of the creaking cupboards. They played like a couple of kids in a toy shop, swapping stories of bargains and bargains that they had missed. In short, Carol was like a dose of medicine to her and became a close friend. She offered me the chance to speak to her when I needed to, and I did need to.

Chapter 22. Blue Badge

Our living habits did not change at that early stage of her illness, I continued to be the Head Cook and Bottlewasher, Pam stayed as elegant an stylish as always, we went shopping together, we paid visits to our beloved Epping Forest and of course we visited our large brood of children and grandchildren and they visited us. Eventually she became tired after such small outings, so I would leave her in the car whilst I did the shopping. Not an ideal situation!

I then applied for a Blue Badge to aid with our parking problems. These badges were notoriously difficult to get in Hackney, but I simply went into the office where they are issued from. Because Pam was having difficulty walking and there is no parking outside this huge building I took a cab that parked right outside the office. Many tales have been told of the strictness of the examiners and the trickery that they indulge in, so I prepared myself for an argument at least. I had bought Pam a walking stick, one of those with a tasteful pattern on it. It so happened that this stick blended in with the attractive outfit that Pam had chosen for the visit. We sat outside of the office on a bench, as we sat there I rehearsed my plea for the precious Blue Badge, I even thought of kicking up a stink if anyone made things difficult for us. Whatever I planned was unnecessary because within a short couple of minutes the door opened and there stood a smiling Irish lady who welcomed us in to her roomy office. "Oh you do look so nice" said our delightful host, "even your walking stick matches your lovely outfit" Then turning to me she told me what a smart appearance that I had. I noted that she watched us with intensity as I helped Pam overcome her problem with walking. She gently explained what would happen in this interview then she moved from behind her desk and sat next to the nervous Pam and held her hand. I'm sure this was not council procedure, just the reaction of this special, kind hearted lady. When she was finished with us I called a cab and she offered to take Pam to the picking up point. "Can I hold your arm?" asked Pam. "Of course my dear" said our kind and thoughtful host. As Pam held her arm our new found admirer, she added "Oh, my dear you are so weak" I felt that Pam was in good and sympathetic hands and Pam looked pleased to be with her new friend, but I watched closely as the pair of them looked unsteady. Our lovely Irish host made Pam comfortable in the cab then leaned in and gave her a gentle peck on the cheek.

Stepping out of the cab she came to me and advised me that the result of this interview would go before a panel of specialists and we would hear from them in about six weeks. Just two days later there was a loud flop as a heavy piece of mail dropped through our letter box. It was of course, Pam's Blue Badge.

Her love of glamour was still important to her so every morning I would get her makeup bag and let her put her always immaculate 'face' on. But one morning this ritual turned into a disaster, she sat putting her well practiced street face on, as usual she asked me if she looked good, but when I cast my eye on her beautiful features I caught my breath. I had long admired her ability to paint her eyebrows on in such a skilful way, with no trouble at all she would take the pencil and produce two absolutely perfect arcs, then apply her eye shadow in the most tasteful way making her lovely features look even more lovely, but this day was drastically different. The eyebrows were completely different and out of place, her eye shadow was daubed on again in the wrong place. I felt my eyes begin to moisten because my very particular Pam resembled a clown. If it wasn't so sad I would have laughed. In her usual way she looked at me and asked my approval of her usually skilful application of her 'war paint' as she called it, smiling at me to make herself just a bit more attractive. But this time I was filled with sadness and pity, my beauty had lost her natural dignity, I tried to hold back the tears but with no success. We still slept together enjoying our nightly cuddles and good night kisses, we were still as in love as we were as youngsters and were never afraid to say it. At this time the scariest and most worrying occurrences happened. Pam started seeing things and people who were just not there. She would wake me in the middle of the night in a frightened state to tell me that someone was in the other room and insisted that I should get up and tell them to go. Of course I would enter the room, with just a little bit of uncertainty, perhaps there was someone there, but of course the room was empty but she would insist that we had an unwanted visitor, so I just told her that it was the shadow of the curtain. Sometimes two men dressed in black were standing in the hall or a man was sitting in the armchair in our bedroom. One sunny Sunday our son Glenn and his wife Joanne visited us, the doors to the garden were wide open to give Pam a good view of the garden and the birds on the bird feeder, when she called me "Look Brian, your girlfriend is in the garden, you know that black lady, she does look nice in her green dress, such a good looking woman" Of course the garden was empty but she insisted that 'my girl friend' had brought along all of her many kids. When Glenn went to look in the garden she said that he had lots of earwigs in his hair, a chill ran down my spine and I closed the doors putting an end to this particular delusion. Such strange occurrences carried on but the worst was yet to come. She often told me about her friend 'Brian' who strangely looked just like me, he had a beard like mine, hair like mine and spoke like me. I would tell her something and the following day she would tell it to me. When I asked her how did she know that, she would answer "Brian told me, not you but the other Brian" I'm afraid the other Brian gave me the creeps and made my stomach churn and strangely made me just a bit jealous. One night as I got out of the bath, she scrutinised me from head to toe declaring that the other Brian had a body just like mine and even had a tattoo just like me. I found this to be incredibly eerie. It seemed that the woman that I loved so much was disappearing into a strange and unknown world.

As if this wasn't enough she began to be perturbed when ever she entered our smaller bedroom, she would shake with fear because ' There were lots of people in there, people of all nationalities and they were all squashed together and making a noise, one of them was a ballet dancer' she explained. I went into the room but saw nothing. This occurred four or five times, I was perplexed and worried that she may be getting worse, what would happen next? I was so worried that I went into this cursed room, closed the door and took a long look around, and then the answer became clear. On the wall I had hung a collection of photos of our many grandchildren, I had done this years ago when they were very young. There for all to see was our multicultural brood, all looking jolly and the ballet mistress was our granddaughter Rebekah, when she was three years old dressed in ballet clothes complete with ballet shoes that were bound up her legs. Pam had seen her beloved grandchildren in a different way and had given her own interpretation to this dated but loving tribute to our small kids. When I explained what I had found to Pam she accepted it and was never troubled by these photos again. I was upset when I thought of the fear and confusion these lovely family photos brought to her.

A few other weird events happened that I will not divulge.

Chapter 23. The Spanish Wedding

At this time my son Bill announced that he and his girlfriend Elsa were going to be married. They were both overjoyed and Bill, never one for doing things by half, had invited half of Southern Britain to the wedding. Just to make the tale more complicated Elsa was Spanish, not any ordinary Spanish but a full bred Basque. Basques are a unique people with their own language and traditions and an unknown ancestry. The problem was that wedding was to be held in Basque territory in Northern Spain, 'Just a couple of hours flight' said Bill simply forgetting that his mum was ill and having difficulty travelling. This frightened the life from me and made me think of all the disastrous things that could possibly happen to my dear Pam. Bill reassured me and seeing that a large consignment of the Walker family would be with us I felt just a tiny bit safer. We had a wheelchair for Pam and the airline looked after her during the pleasant flight, loading and unloading her by means of a hoist, I think that she loved the attention that the airline workers making such a fuss of her made her think that she was someone special, well we all thought that she was, so no argument there!

The wedding ceremony was to be held in a lovely little unspoilt town called Elorrio and Bill had found us an ideal little hotel in the mountains just outside of the town. The view from our bedroom window was of high rugged mountains and blue skies and the food strictly Basque, It was Ideal, except for Pam's illness, The evenings were dark and quiet making Pam very nervous but our son John was with us and being his mum's favourite, he helped to calm her down. In this small hotel the breakfasts were prepared the night before so guests simply helped themselves, made tea and entered the dining room to eat the lovely healthy food. I awoke early, Pam was still asleep, so knowing her preference for Tea in Bed, I quietly slipped out of our room and into the kitchen brewed up her tea and returned to the bedroom, but I never arrived at our rustic boudoir because I met my delicate Pam wandering along the passage with a very distressed look upon her face. I felt so upset to see her in such a turmoiled state. Both John and me reassured her and gave her the tea. It was so plain to see the mental agony on her face.

Later as we prepared for the wedding she brightened up a little bit and with Joanne helping her to beautify herself she started to show us her special smile. We took a taxi to the town centre and the Town Hall where the wedding was to be held. This was in the centre of town, it was so Spanish. What Bill had not told us was that this was the day of the local Fiesta and the place was full of good looking smart women, I am here to tell you that even in her wheelchair she looked stunning and attracted so much admiration, so many people took photos of her.

After the fastest wedding ceremony ever, the square was full of dancing Fiesta goers, Pam had that special look on her face, I was so happy for her that I gave her a kiss, mind you, I had to queue for it, because everyone admired her so much that they formed a line. The taxi driver who looked after us was a woman who taught in a local college, she was young and spoke perfect English, her natural charm was there for all to see. Pam was not feeling as well as she would like to be but soon felt better when our cab driver attended to her, helping her in and out of the cab and speaking very encouragingly to Pam, 'The Mother of the Bridegroom'. When we left this little bit of paradise this lovely young woman named Aurkene, came to say good-bye to us, she wished Pam well and kissed her good-bye and to my surprise she kissed me too. I can honestly say that was the one and only time that I had been kissed a by a Taxi driver. The return flight to Stanstead was uneventful so Pam slept a lot of the way, but when she woke she did have a fretful look upon her face.

As time went by Pam's tiredness turned to discomfort and eventually pain, her healthy glow faded and her special smile was seldom seen.

All this time, loyal Joanne kept Pam happy with endless 'phone calls, daily visits and best of all juicy gossip. Of course our three sons kept a watchful eye on us all, helping with the daily duties around the house but most important of all, loving their Mum. Instead of taking her shopping as usual Joanne would buy her even more fashionable clothes online knowing full well that they would be returned. Anything that we needed our boys got for us.

Then her tiredness turned to an inability to walk, this difficulty gave me problems, I could hold her up to get around the house but she never wanted to move much so there was not too much of a problem with this. We had a stair lift fitted and she quite liked riding up and down on this, but never took much care of herself whilst riding on it. She would quite often have one of her trade-mark long scarfs dangling dangerously near the mechanism frightening the life out of me and making me lose my temper because she didn't remember to check that she was safe, but of course she just couldn't, any way that was my job to do. This just made me feel guilty, because all those years ago I promised to look after and care for her.

I bought her a wheelchair so that I could take her shopping and walking, but by now we were eighty years old and pushing a chair and my precious load was no longer easy for me. One day I was pushing Pam and her wheelchair through our local market when a woman spied her and with a shocked look on her face darted through the traffic, as she neared us she burst into tears, hugging and smothering Pam with kisses and saying "Pam, Dear Pam, what has happened to you?" This woman was the young girl that Pam had befriended when she worked in the Children's Home all those years ago, Pam had often told me of the pitiful life that this woman had as a little girl and of how they both became close and this woman almost regarded Pam as her mother. Both Pam and this woman wept and I am not ashamed to say that I joined in.

It is widely known that Pam is a paid-up member of the Marks and Spencer's Appreciation Society and she was missing her shopping trips with Joanne or one of the other daughters-in-law. She made it known to me that she would love to visit a lovely M & S Super Store, so I loaded the wheelchair into the car and headed through the Blackwall Tunnel to Greenwich. At Greenwich is a vast new shopping park and right in the middle is the thing that my dear old Pam wanted the most, a brand new, multi storey, shiny Marks and Spencer's Superstore. Her face lit up when she saw it, her impossible dreams had come true. I pushed her wheelchair into the first door that I could see and we found ourselves in the food hall, "I don't want anything in here she said, but wait a minute, let me have a look at the foodstuff before we look at the clothes" So we meandered around the huge food hall going backward and forwards many times and coming out with a couple of items that she wasn't sure that we wanted.

Then we went in the elevator up to the Women's clothing department. Her face wore a big smile just like a kid in a sweet shop, only she wasn't after sweets but something more stylish. I pushed her around the many lanes of dresses, trousers, underwear, and shoes, then she said "Take me round again, there was some 'bits and pieces' that I liked over there, or was it over there? By now my ancient legs were crying for a rest and the central heating was not to my liking, so I suggested a break. There were no chairs to sit on so I found a base of a display and plonked my weary body on to it, causing the mannequin to sway from side to side. Pam sat in the wheelchair looking uncomfortable.

Just then I saw the floor manager approaching me with a determined look on her face. "Are you alright sir?" she asked so I explained my predicament to her so she took me to a small showroom with a comfortable armchair for me to rest my wobbly legs. "Where is my wife ?" I asked the now pleasant manager. "Don't worry my colleague is looking after her, why don't you rest here while we take her around our stock" What a relief! I settled down in my cosy chair and saw the two charming ladies chatting away to Pam as they pushed the wheelchair with the greatest of ease. About an hour later all three returned, Pam had a neat pile of clothes on her lap and one of our angelic helpers was holding her hand. Pam just loved it!

I thanked this special couple of thoughtful helpers but felt sad that I could not look after Pam myself. Although I was not to blame for anything I felt that everything was my fault, but worse was to come.

Soon after, Pam was virtually housebound and spent most of her time in the front room laid out on our large, comfortable sofa. Her legs were now weak but I could hold her up as she shuffled a short distance to the lavatory or to the stairlift. Her bowels were now affected and it became necessary to put disposable pants on her, a job that I had difficulty with so it was time to seek help with caring for her. With just a few 'phone calls and questions and of course with the help of Joanne, we were given a carer to help Pam with her washing and dressing, twice a day. I was pleased but apprehensive about having an outsider coming into our home and sharing the loss of Pam's dignity, but my concern was ill-founded as I found out on the first visit. The carer entered our home as if she had been there many times, in my ignorance and my care for my precious Pam I had underestimated her professionalism, but I should have known that Pam's charm, which was still working it's magic, would get around any such obstacle. This carer was called Eylem and was Turkish. Pam couldn't wait to tell her of our Turkish grandchildren and Eylem remarked that she liked Pam's makeup and hair, "We don't get many clients that look as glamorous as you" said the admiring Eylem, of course they both became friends from the start. Eylem was so caring and affectionate to Pam and after a couple of days we discovered why. It seems that when Pam was a crafts Teacher, Eylem was one of her pupils. Eylem kept looking at Pam and asked if she was the Mrs. Walker who taught her, Pam of course answered yes and Eylem got very emotional and hugged and kissed her much admired Mrs. Walker, there were moist eyes as Eylem explained that when Pam ran the tuck shop, Eylem when buying penny sweets would ask Pam to pick out the strawberry flavoured chews because she liked them best and of course the kind hearted Pam would oblige by sorting out the favourite sweets for the very young Eylem. More kisses and admiration from the wonderful Eylem and more affection whenever she called. See, I did tell you that Pam was special.

Pam's ability to walk was waning but I managed to support her to the toilet and to the chairlift and although she was losing weight rapidly I was not getting younger or stronger. My concern for her made me lose weight and strength but I did not admit it even to myself and a couple of nights when taking her from her downstairs sofa up to bed I struggled. She had reached the point where her legs were just not working at all and all her weight was placed upon me to shift, eventually the chore became impossible for me, but stubborn old bugger that I am, I just could not admit it, and my precious cargo simply slipped through my arms and on to the floor, I was mortified! It was late at night and I had no-one to call so I got blankets and pillows and settled us down on the floor to spend the night. I tried to tell Pam that it was 'Just like camping' but it wasn't at all. Pam and I both had a very uncomfortable night and again I felt very ashamed about putting Pam into such dangerous situation. The following day I told our nearby neighbours, Sue and Clive, about my stupid behaviour and they reprimanded me, gave me their phone number and made my promise not to be such an idiot again. Well they didn't have to wait too long because that night the same thing happened again, but this time I immediately called Sue and Clive, who came across the road still dressed in their pyjamas to rescue us all over again. Then Sue tenderly tucked Pam into her bed and she kissed her goodnight making me tearful yet again,

Now it was plain to see that our hopes of recovery were absolutely ill founded. She became even weaker and restless, but she never lost her sense of style and glamour. Every day she applied her skin nourishment and carefully put her make up on. Her hair was brushed daily but as her strength dwindled she found it difficult to be exact with her eyebrow pencil and lipstick, but she firmly forbade me to lay a hand on her makeup bag.

All through this period of heart-breaking events Pam was burdened with ill health, she had developed bowel problems of a severe kind. She went into hospital several times for tests and some of these tests were very intrusive and uncomfortable. Pam had a dislike of being 'pulled about' as she described it but she now seemed unaware of the discomfort and indignity of the tests, or perhaps she had come to terms with the suffering. Most of these tests were in our own area and in our own Homerton University Hospital, but now and then in the London Hospital in Whitechapel. Where-ever they were they drained her of her energy.

At the time of these tests Pam was in our own home and being treated by her own G.P. Dr.Gohl, ably represented by Dr.Goni. As Pam could no longer move about, the gallant Dr.Goni would come to our house to tend to this special but now delicate patient. We hear stories of patients being kept waiting for doctors to arrive but the very positive and likeable Dr.Goni knocked on the door within ten minutes of a call to the Surgery. He addressed us by our first names and soon became a friend and a saviour to us. I have lost count of the number of visits made by Dr.Goni and of the treatments meted out by him. We developed a system of getting the medicines in a hurry. In her work for the local G.P. Pam worked closely with our local pharmacy and was given extra helpful treatment by the pharmacist, Abbe and his team. Abbe became a good person to have on our side in troubled times and with a certain amount of co-operation moved things along when needed.

It was now clear that my lovely Pam was slowly sinking, I did not want to think about it too much and still had a hope that she would recover and that we would live happily ever after, after all she was my special love, so nothing could happen to her. Could it?

Pam was now bed ridden and with the undying attention from Eylem and her loyal team of carers we set up a care room in our spare room. The Homerton Hospital provided us with a hospital bed and other equipment to make the caring more agreeable. They sent a commode that we saw as old fashioned and a burden but it was found to be helpful in the caring for my poor suffering Pam.

In spite of being more comfortable in her own little room at home her health deteriorated rapidly, after yet more tests and examinations she was taken into Homerton Hospital and placed into The Older Age Group ward. Of course she never knew, or even cared about sharing a ward with all these older patients, most of whom were in fact a lot younger than Pam. She continued to carry out her usual preparation to her bright and still beautiful face making her look like she had been placed in the wrong ward. She was much admired by the nurses and patients who spoke to her as they passed her bed, this gave Pam a feeling of happiness and brought on one of her special smiles thus spreading the feeling of 'things are not so bad now.' However she was not getting any better and still in considerable discomfort, so more tests and examinations that revealed absolutely nothing! By now she was so weak and unwell that she finally gave up her daily make-up routine when something quite marvellous and very moving happened, the nurses on this ward so used to seeing at her glamorous best, put her make-up on for her, combed her hair and made sure that she had clean pyjamas on. They clearly had feelings of admiration for her.

Then she was transferred to The Mary Seacole Nursing Home which I saw as an indication that they had no more treatment for her. This small but cosy home was so quiet with each patient having a room of their own, very good but a bit lonely for those who liked a bit of company.

As Christmas approached we made preparation to take Pam home for a few days and soon an ambulance did indeed bring her home. I was very concerned for her welfare because now she was very weak and uncomfortable. With the help of our family we got her into her room and sat with her day and night, we all knew that the end was near but no-one wanted to say it.

On Christmas day we managed to take her to Joanne's house for Christmas dinner and she did in fact eat well and enjoyed it, even managing one of her much-admired smiles that made us all feel happy. As soon as our festive lunch was over we rushed our delicate Pam home to her own room and the comfort of her own bed. She was not expected back to Mary Seacole Home for a few days and this spare time was not wasted because a steady flow of visitors came to visit her. This was probably the best thing to happen at this unplanned time. Friends, neighbours, family, ex-workmates all called in to visit her for a chat, bringing joy and love to her. Of course we all knew that they were coming to say goodbye to this special, iconic woman, knowing that it may be their last chance to see her, but somehow it was not a tragic mood that they brought with them but more like an impromptu tea party. The party goers were all pleased to see her and brought little treats and messages from their families but best of all one or two items of gossip that had Pam grinning from ear to ear. She more than once joined in with the gossip making these women only parties laugh out loud, it was better than all the medicines in the world to see her so happy. Our close neighbour Sue came at least three times just to join in with the chat and loving friendship. Lifelong friends like Linda, Camilla and Michelle added to the membership of this unique nightly event and provided the things that Pam was lacking, affection and love and of course a bit more of the gossip, I'm sure that some of this gossip was manufactured just to make Pam happy. Whatever it was I was happy to let these good friends just get on with their own brand of Tea Parties by just simply lifting a lot of the gloom from all the party guests.

After the festive holidays, as we predicted she was returned to The Mary Seacole Nursing Home, she was now looking weaker than ever before so we made a rota of close family to be with her all the time. Of course the early rising Joanne started the daily routine with a visit at eight o'clock, then I would visit after Joanne left until John arrived about four o'clock in the afternoon. Then Bill and his wife arrived around five or six o'clock. Pam was by now very weak and sometimes unresponsive or asleep but we all held her hand and talked to her, sometimes she answered, sometimes not. Of course we all brought little titbits and treats for her but not many of them were eaten, once a week I would collect the tiny tokens of our love and ignoring my feelings throw them in the bin. Sweets, bars of chocolate, crisps and fruit just simply withered away making an unhappy and a not very hygienic sight, but Pam could never even notice that they had been brought in.

But our teenage love was still alive somewhere, each night when I left her I would say "Goodnight Pam, I love you" and she would answer "I love you too"

By now her speech was slurred and weak but it was plain that she was able to make out who was with her and roughly know what was said. One night, after she had been moaning and complaining I arrived and she held my hand and smiled at me. The senior nurse said to her "Pamela, the only time that I see you smile is when Brian arrives" Pam with a very feeble tone replied "We have been in love for sixty five years" Nurse smiled but I couldn't talk because I had a very large lump was in my throat. I went home and had a good cry because I now knew just how much we loved each other.

Chapter 24. Goodbye

We kept this nightly vigil all through and beyond January, never once letting the most important member of our family down, I tried to be philosophical about these events but I failed dismally. She was fading away before our eyes and there was nothing that we could do about it.

Many of our friends and family popped in as they said to 'just see her,' but I knew that they were saying 'Goodbye' to her. It was hard to take it all in.

By now her mood was changing, this lovely, gentle lady was now getting just a bit aggressive, not in a physical way but in a verbal way, she was using swear words to everyone. One night I heard her cursing to the Senior Sister and told her not to use such language, Sister said "You should have heard her in the night, I had every letter from A to Z." I apologised but the seasoned nurse said "Don't worry, most of the patients go through this stage" Although this dedicated nurse never took offence to this vile behaviour it upset me, not because I was a delicate minded person but because this beautiful, stylish woman who I had adored for all these years was fading away in front of my eyes and there was nothing that I could do about it. I felt so useless! I sat with her until late, she never spoke a word, but after a long time I kissed and said "Goodnight Pam, I love you!" Without opening her eyes she simply said "Oh Go on F*** Off!" They were the very last words that she ever spoke to me. I know that she never knew what she said but stupidly I felt upset that she could burst my bubble of hope in such a brutal manner.

The following day I visited her again, I entered the tiny room to a silence except for the rasping sound of her breathing, Joanne had been in and told me of her condition.

Later that day our close and dear friend Theresa, known to everyone as Pookie, arrived to 'be with me'. I knew exactly what she meant. We both spoke to Pam and we even sang a couple of songs to her with absolutely no response. Most of the time we simply held her hand but it never seemed to be enough. Later that day Pookie went home and Good old Joanne arrived for her second watch of that day, Joanne looked sad and resigned for the worst. I was just as resigned too, but very tired and in need of a break, so I suggested that we should go home and return in the morning, but the very valiant Joanne said that she would sit with her and phone me 'if anything happens.'

It was now about Nine Thirty and I said goodbye to Pam, gave her a kiss and told her that I loved her. I said Goodnight to Joanne, not knowing if I was doing the right thing or not and drove home. The short journey took just fifteen minutes, and as I approached my door I heard the phone ringing, I lifted it up to hear the voice of Joanne "Is everything all right,?" I asked, but the answer was inevitable. In a serious and dignified way Joanne said "Pam has just passed away" There was a moment of silence as we both searched for words to say to each other, but our silence spoke a thousand words.

Chapter 25. Facing the truth

That night I was alone in our house, just me and my thoughts, I tried to be as positive as I could, but found it impossible to be at ease with what had happened over the last three years. The only positive feeling was that Pam was no longer suffering and would no longer lose her dignity. For some unexplained reason I felt relieved and settled, but not for too long. I couldn't come to terms with her not being with me anymore and had visions of how my special and immaculate Pam would be in a coffin. Would she be comfortable? Would she be frightened? All the things that I had tried to protect her from had tragically happened to her. Not a pleasant thought.

I was not alone for long because Joanne and Glenn arrived looking so tired and sad. Then Bill and Elsa came, they too looked bewildered and drained, I just felt puzzled. What would we do now? John, by far the most sensitive of us disappeared from the whole heart breaking and sad scene. We never knew where he was but we left him alone to grieve on his own. This was the strangest night of the whole tragic event. No prayers, no goodbye speeches just us, a small part of the family quietly remembering our special Mum and Wife while we silently sipped tea. Early the next morning I woke up and had to give myself a reminder of what had happened the night before, it all seemed so unbelievable but of course it was tragically true. I phoned Joanne, she was awake as I had expected and just as lost in sadness as me. I decided to carry on as usual, so easy I thought, but the sympathy of our strong community made it impossible to be ordinary. I strolled across our shopping square and called into the nearest shop, our off-licence and spoke to Florence giving her the sad news, she emerged from behind the counter and hugged me. I saw one of the council workers who immediately took me into the manager's office where Tracy, the manager gave me another hug and then Tony the estate cleaner had heard the news and came to me with sincere sympathy, he felt it necessary to accompany me on my difficult task of informing all our long-time friends.

Most sad and touching of all I entered the local Newsagents and Post Office to tell Hari Patel the owner. Hari had been a long-time admirer of Pam, often asking her why she had married such an ugly man like me when he was willing to marry her, my reply was always the same, "Take a look in the mirror Hari and see the truth". He always made out that he was hard hearted but my sad news told the truth about his tender feelings. He was serving at the till and a long queue of customers were waiting to get served, he asked me if I was O.K. but I told him that Pam had died just a few hours ago. He looked upset and immediately closed the till and stepped outside of the counter, put his arms around me and asked if there was anything that I wanted to help me at this difficult time. I noticed that he was very shocked and surprised by my sad news. Somehow the sympathy and help that I received that morning made me assured of the many friends that I had around.

When Hari had closed the till the long queue of customers just stood without moaning or getting agitated but had sympathy with my family's plight. One young woman, in her thirties, I reckoned, stood silently by listening to me and Hari's sad conversation. I looked at this complete stranger who was crying. The tears were streaming down her fresh cheeks, she never wiped her lovely face and I noticed that these tears glistened like diamonds, If I had been of different beliefs I would have said that this was a sign, of what I don't know.

Now we had to arrange the funeral. This dreaded chore was perhaps the best thing that we could do, it gave us something to concentrate on and get just a little out of the routine of hospitals and care homes. But before this routine of booking the undertakers, the caterers, the printers and most of all someone to conduct the service. As a matter of course we booked the Co-operative Funeral Service. Our family had used this undertaking business for many years but I never thought that I would be discussing my own wife's funeral service and be talking about the intimate details of some-one that I loved so much, it felt so strange. However the young woman we dealt with was warm, friendly, understanding and reassuring, she made this dreaded episode so easy for me and Joanne to bear. All this took place just when the coronavirus had been revealed and quite frankly we didn't take this dreadful disease very seriously. Our booking was the last full funeral to take place before the lockdown rules were applied. In fact one of our close neighbours who had died just a day or two after Pam, was allowed just a handful of mourners to attend the much trimmed down service.

A few days before the service we had a visit from Alex Hall, the Funeral Celebrant, this title was new to me but I was really happy with this because we didn't really want a morbid service, we preferred something that reflected Pam's charm and happiness. We are not religious at all so we never spoke of anything remotely God-like but left a place in the service where those who wanted to could reflect on their own thoughts. Alex was a smart, down to earth man with a fine way with words and a straightforward attitude.

We had asked the mourners to dress in a happy but stylish manner to reflect Pam's unique style of dressing, we also asked for those who attended this unique event to wear something in animal print to pay homage to her trademark style. Fortunately, as we were waiting for the cortege to arrive Joanne found a large box absolutely filled with Pam's vast collection of scarves of every style, Pam would buy anything that caught her eye when she was shopping and invariably simply lay them very carefully in this large cardboard carton. This find was perfect, we handed them out to neighbours and in fact anyone who showed an interest, the vast remainder were taken to the Crematorium to be handed out to the congregation. I was very moved to see neighbours holding the scarves and wiping their eyes. Our next-door neighbours, who are very close and loving friends but could not attend the service because of disability, sobbed very loudly, Zehra the mother and Pam's close friend covered her face with her hands and wept unashamedly. Her daughter, Shifa, was just as overcome wiping her eyes and telling everyone that "Dear Pam was just like a mother to me!"

The cortege slowly pulled out of our road and glided its way to the Crematorium. During the journey not much was said. Just a strange kind of silence that was unusual for our very talkative family. The cortege reached the chapel with the coffin arriving last. As the mourners entered, they were offered a scarf which they accepted with pleasure, even the undertakers bedecked themselves in Pam's immaculate and stylish accessories. The whole event now a had a touch of the many festivals that we had been involved in and smiles replaced the sombre faces, just what we wanted.

Then for me the most sentimental part of the event, when the congregation were all in and seated the coffin was brought in. The whole place fell silent.

We had seven grandsons standing by ready to carry their beloved Nan to the curtained entrance to her final resting place, we were expecting to have eight bearers but only four were needed but my very gentlemanly grandsons just respectfully took their places and not a sound was heard. I was so proud of them. These bearers, my grandsons, are all full grown men and have grown up to be rather manly and quite tough looking, but as I glanced over my shoulder they were all standing in a line, each one weeping for their Nanny. Of course I joined in.

The celebrant mounted the podium and addressed the congregation. He had visited me the previous week and we had an enjoyable hour talking about Pam and her life and of course our love for each other, about her scary childhood, her skills, her loving personality and her beauty. Although he had only seen photos of her he described her as being like a film star, but who was I to argue with him? He then invited Joanne to speak, she spoke of her closeness and love for Pam and said that she loved her like she was her real mum. But the best response was to a remark about Pam buying many clothes and taking them back. Then our son Bill spoke of her kindness and love that she lavished upon our kids and her grandchildren and of his love for his special Mum.

Then our eldest grandson James had memories of being very young and the regular Saturday nights that he spent with Nanny when she over-did the love and attention that she gave to her first grandchild. He was full of emotion when he spoke of the fun that we had as a family.

We had some of Pam's favourite music and a minute's silence for her.

About two hundred people attended the service for their friend, sister, neighbour and admirer. Of course, it was sad but not at all sombre as many of her friends and admirers chatted about her and her beauty and style, I found it all so satisfying and touching. We all went outside to the lawn and admired the wreathes and tributes. Many of the congregation came to me with messages of commiseration. A few close friends hugged me and promised to keep an eye on me in the near future and one dear friend came and although he was sad he patted his jacket and said that he had fetched 'Three Grand for me' in case I never had enough money. I never accepted this very old-fashioned but satisfying East End gesture from a special mate.

After the service we all moved across the road to the nearby pub where a fine display of food was laid on for us. Suddenly all the tension and sadness seemed to float away and we could all say Goodbye to Our Pam in a respectful way. I went around as many people as I could to say Thank you for coming. I'm not sure if I got to everyone, but if I missed you- 'Thank You!'

After the funeral I took a cab home and entered my house fully expecting to see my lovely Pam complete with her special smile, but of course she wasn't there. I know that I had been on my own for some time while Pam was being tended by the dedicated nurses, but now the house seemed so empty and lonely and the truth suddenly hit me, she wasn't going to return. Looking back to it now what did

I expect? Certainly not this blank feeling or the fear of loneliness. This was the time that I began to talk to her, I do it most night and it brings me much satisfaction. Let me say now that I don't believe in spirits, ghosts, the here-after or angels and I certainly don't believe in God, but now I firmly believe in the power of love, Pam has died but our lifelong love lives on and makes me feel close to her. We are still a couple and I hope that we will always be. I am now eighty-two, a bit doddery and forgetful but I hope that me and the glorious Pamela will be together for as long as we can. I simply Love her.

Once that the funeral and the legal matters had been attended to I concentrated on tying up the loose ends. Of course a delightful and popular person like Pam had many tributes sent to her, I had read them all and had wept but there they lay, a bit like yesterday's newspapers but when I read them again the tears flowed. Such tributes from so many people, such love and sadness poured out by so many people, I just couldn't help but wipe my eyes for a second time.

There are too many to be included here but this one arrived a bit after the others at a time when our tears were settling down. It was from a close neighbour. Her name is Hira, she is from a Pakistani family who have lived close to us for many years, the children and grandchildren of this family have very respectfully addressed both me and Pam as Mr. Brian and Miss Pam. The writer of this letter has always been described by me as a little girl, but when I wasn't looking she suddenly became thirty-five years old. She is shy and charming. This is what she wrote:

Dear Mr. Brian,

With a heavy heart and a lack of words, I write to you.

The news of Miss Pam was given to me by my family and honestly I felt an ache, for the loss of Miss Pam and for you losing her.

I have known you both for the whole of my life and have considered you family,

I have the utmost respect and love for you both, this time is one at which nothing can be said or given to fill the gaping void, I always saw how beautifully and wonderfully you spoke of Miss Pam. I loved it. I wish I could have spent more time with you both, and I will always try.

You are in my prayers and thoughts, I'm sorry it has taken me this long to come and see you.

With love, Hira x

Chapter 26. Back to normal?

Back to normal?? Whatever that meant? Now that the funeral was over, what next? I had somehow not thought about my new but unwelcome life. I had no idea of what I wanted to do, or how I would get on by myself. Of course I felt that there may be some advantage to being on my own, I could now do whatever I wanted to but the snag was that I couldn't think of anything that didn't involve Pam. The thought of going on a holiday on my own revolted me and even a day by the sea seemed ridiculous. I am now past my prime and my beloved garden has become a bit too much for me. I told myself to liven up and get on with it. I had always had great pleasure in getting my hands dirty and keeping the garden as attractive as I could, in fact I had won two gold prizes in the local gardening competition so that seemed to be the way to go, but my first attempts to work the flower beds exhausted me and made me realize that my gardening days were over. I had suffered a small stroke a few months before and I was very optimistic that I would get over the damage that was inflicted on me. So bloody disappointing now to find that I had no skills left. Somehow I felt guilty that I could not do much.

The house seems so much more empty and I feel lonely most days, but I have Pam to talk to, not that she could hear me, but, strangely, talking to her helps me. Every night I say Good Night to her and tell her that I love her and tell her of family events. Joanne and Glenn have recently moved out of London and I went to the new house and came back to make a full report to her. Do I think that I have mental problems? Not one bit, I realise that she is no longer with me but I still need her to talk to, I hope that she will never leave me. When I was in the army one of my room mates was a big Scotsman who had a tattoo right across his mighty chest. It read "TRUE LOVE NEVER DIES". At the time I thought that it was soppy and not very original, but now I think that it is so true!

The future? Just after we lost her I was undecided about what I would do, I considered, travelling, meeting new friends, catching up with old friends and joining a club of some kind. I was never one for formality and I do not suffer fools kindly. So, this is why I am here, writing about my romantic life with Pam, my love for her and loss of her. What happens next is not in my hands, I am pretty ancient now, not in the best of health and lonely. So I am not too worried about the future, why should I be? I have had a life blessed with my beautiful, stylish, feminine sweetheart, I can't ask for more.

Goodnight Pam. I love you.

Tributes

While Pam was ill she received such sympathetic and kind actions from many people. I would like to thank the following groups and individuals.

The Alzheimer's Society, for the help and assistance that they gave us.

The Lea Surgery with Dr.Gohl, DrGoni and the rest of the staff, many of whom knew her work as a doctor's receptionist.

The Mary Seacole Nursing Home and their sympathetic nurses and staff.

Of course our own Homerton University Hospital and the nurses and Doctors. They were so professional and kind even putting Pam's make up on her when she could not do it herself. As a family we spent quite a lot of time there, never once getting anything but help and understanding from the medical staff, some of them became friends of ours. Not forgetting the cleaning and catering staff, the ambulance workers, the security staff and everyone who helped us in this tragic time.

The friends, that we have in Regal Pharmacy, Chatsworth Road. Abbe the Pharmacist went out of his way to help us, many times working at the last minute to prepare the medication and delivering them to our door. The staff, many of whom that we had known for years certainly became our friends and loved Pam.

Hackney Social Services. Thanks to Emma and the team.

The biggest thanks goes to our precious National Health Service, please protect it and be grateful for it. Don't let anyone misuse it, demolish it or sell it off.

The Co-op Funeral service for making this difficult period so easy for our family, to the many friends, neighbours and sympathisers who gave as so much support.

Finally I must tell you of my local Pharmacy, Bees Pharmacy in Rushmore road. They were not Pam's pharmacists, but mine, they watched over me in my more troubled days and offered advice and most of all friendship. Rita, Samson and their very pleasant assistants never failed to help me when I needed it.

Thanks to our dependable neighbours, Sue and Clive Clark, Linda O'Connor, Michelle and Jon and their two lovely children, Camilla Philips for her constant care about me and to my niece Clare Smith. She never fails to tell me that she loves me, she is the only one to still call me Uncle Brian, it's all a bit dated now but I love it.

To Alan Rossitter for without failure comes every week for coffee and cake and a good old chat.

A big emotional thanks to our families, both mine and Pam's for listening to our tales of woe and standing by us. Over the many years it has become difficult to remember just what part of the family some people are from, we have become one big sympathetic tribe.

The Doctors and staff at the Athena Medical Centre, a special thanks to Dr. Cleaton for her regular calls to me just to see if I am well.

To Dr.Shui for ordering me to write this book. Her kindness and understanding encouraged me into action when I needed it.

A big thanks to Pam's two remaining sisters, Patricia and Janice. Both have ill health in their families, but still remembered to be helpful and supportive to Pam and me.

The biggest and best tribute that I can give is to the person who never quavered in her love and attention that she gave to Pam ,Joanne Walker, our daughter in law. She was there whenever we needed her, early in the morning, in the middle of the night or even staying through the night to tend to her 'Lovely Mother in Law.' She organised all Pam's many appointments, liaised with the health workers, organised the funeral, did a bit of shopping when we needed it and even kept an eye on me. She could never take any kind of compliment, when I recently suggested that she should receive a medal for 'Services Over and Above the Call of Duty'', she just rolled her eyes and told me to "Shut up".

The Last Farewell

Pam was cremated and her ashes stored in the City of London Cemetery. Sometime later we were informed that we could collect her remains and take them wherever we wanted to, or we were offered the opportunity to scatter them in the Garden of Remembrance. It was not an easy choice to make. I had it in the back of my mind to romantically take her to our special place, Epping Forest. But I could not feel comfortable with either place- in truth I just didn't want to say goodbye to her.

Because of the anti-virus precautions we decided to keep the number of people attending the last service to just two of us, Glenn and myself, bidding our special mum and wife farewell. Glenn picked a lovely Red Tree to sprinkle the ashes.

We both left the cemetery in silence.